THE VOCABULARY OF
FIRST-GRADE CHILDREN

THE VOCABULARY OF FIRST-GRADE CHILDREN

By

Alden J. Moe, Ph.D.

Purdue University

Carol J. Hopkins, Ph.D.

Purdue University

R. Timothy Rush, Ph.D.

Indiana University at Kokomo

With a Foreword by

JOHN M. KEAN, Ph.D.
University of Wisconsin

CHARLES C THOMAS • PUBLISHER
Springfield • Illinois • U.S.A.

Published and Distributed Throughout the World by

CHARLES C THOMAS • PUBLISHER

2600 South First Street

Springfield, Illinois 62717, U.S.A.

© *1982 by* CHARLES C THOMAS • PUBLISHER

ISBN 0-398-04623-9

Library of Congress Catalog Card Number: 81-14330

With *THOMAS BOOKS careful attention is given to all details of
manufacturing and design. It is the Publisher's desire to present books that are
satisfactory as to their physical qualities and artistic possibilities and
appropriate for their particular use. THOMAS BOOKS will be true to those
laws of quality that assure a good name and good will.*

Printed in the United States of America

I-RX-1

Library of Congress Cataloging in Publication Data

Moe, Alden J.
    The vocabulary of first-grade children.

    Bibliography: p.
    Includes index.
    1. Children--Language. 2. First grade (Education)
I. Hopkins, Carol J. II. Rush, R. Timothy. III. Title.
LB1139.L3M65   372.6   81-14330
ISBN 0-398-04623-9   AACR2

To

Christine Marie Moe
Perry Wayne Moe
Timothy Edward Hopkins
Emily Christine Hopkins
Tobias Nathaniel Rush
Amity Marie Rush

FOREWORD

THE language of young children has fascinated us for decades. We have examined the syntax, the meanings communicated and the language strategies children use. Understanding the language of children not only enables us to facilitate learning, but provides the incremental knowledge needed to better understand how we all communicate — how we use language to control, inform, imagine, ritualize or express feeling.

Knowledge of the words that children use and the contexts in which they use them has enabled us to prepare educational programs, and to develop teaching techniques that reflect children's language competence. Ever since we learned that word meanings evolve, that they are dynamic rather than static formations, we have recognized the importance of knowing what words are used by children, in what contexts and with what frequency. Our knowledge in these areas has been provided through many case studies and compilations of word lists combined from several studies. But the debate over children's effective repertoire of words and their use of words continues.

As part of their on-going work with child language, Moe, Hopkins, and Rush have added much to our knowledge of what words first grade children do use. First grade children do *know* and *use* a large number of words. Simply to know that in interviews with 329 children, 6,412 different words were used provides impressive support for the necessity to use children's language in our work with them. Such information can provide support for language experience programs, and reinforce the seriousness of the questions about primary reading materials that underestimate children's language facility. The availability of the total corpus of words from the interviews with these 329 children in both alphabetical and frequency order can greatly assist educators, authors, and researchers as they work with children or strive to improve their understanding of how children learn.

Even during the short period in which I had the manuscript, I had occasion to use it several times, once to compare some language samples of fourth grade learning-disabled students, several times to verify guesses about vocabulary being used in some test materials for first grade children, and several times simply to provide examples of subordinating words that are used by first grade children.

The lists themselves, as I have noted, are a needed contribution to the study of children's language. In addition the authors have provided descriptions of their methodology which would allow teachers and researchers to generate their own word lists for comparison purposes. They have shown how computers can be used effectively to analyze, in a relatively short period of time, enormous amounts of text. Further, they have provided a succinct chapter describing ways that their lists can be useful in reading, writing, and spelling. Several sub analyses of the words have also been included. A teacher who wanted to test his or her own student's knowledge based on the frequency lists would find it easy to pull the most frequent words from the list.

The Vocabulary of First-Grade Children is a useful document, useful for its cooroborative information about vocabulary as well as the wealth of new information it contains. All who are interested in children and their language will find this book on vocabulary use an excellent resource. We must help children acquire a multitude of words. Knowing what they already use can only make the task easier.

John M. Kean
University of Wisconsin

PREFACE

THIS book is about the oral vocabulary of first-grade children. Specifically, it presents words spoken by over 300 children and collected during a seven-year period.

The book was written for those individuals who are interested in the words children speak. We believe that the information provided here will be of special interest to students and teachers involved in language arts and reading instruction. Authors and editors of materials for primary-level instruction may also find the information useful. If other audiences find this volume helpful to them, we will, of course, be pleased.

Space does not permit us to name the dozens of teachers and principals who have assisted us during the last seven years, but we thank them and hope that they will be pleased with our final product. We also thank the children and their parents, for they provided the raw material.

Finally, the work presented in this volume is the responsibility of the authors.

A.J.M.
C.J.H.
R.T.R.

CONTENTS

THE VOCABULARY OF
FIRST-GRADE CHILDREN

Chapter I

INTRODUCTION

*T*HE *Vocabulary of First-Grade Children,* the words first-grade students speak, was compiled during the seven-year period from 1974 to 1981 while the authors were engaged in studies of child language. In some of the studies, obtaining the words children spoke was the primary objective. In other studies, the words children spoke became a by-product of the investigations. In all cases, however, one or more of the authors collected the oral language that became the basis for the vocabulary reported in this book.

In all of the studies conducted, language samples were obtained at different times throughout the first-grade year. The language samples from over 300 children were then transcribed, keypunched for computer analysis, and analyzed through the use of computer programs that provided both frequency and alphabetical listings of the words processed. This language provided the 6,412 different words that constitute the vocabulary presented in this book.

This introductory chapter provides a rationale for the work of the authors. It also provides a review of studies previously reported by the authors, which provided information for this book.

CHILD LANGUAGE STUDY

The language of young children is typically studied for several reasons. Child and developmental psychologists are usually interested in what kind of language is exhibited and at what chronological age or developmental stage. The early work of McCarthy (1930), who studied twenty children at half-year intervals between ages eighteen and fifty-four months, provided standards of language collection and analysis that were used throughout the 1930s and 1940s. Investigations by Templin (1957) and Menyuk (1969) provided extensive information concerning the developmental stages of language growth among elementary children, particularly primary-level students. However, the most descriptive information on child language was reported by Brown (1973), who studied Adam, Eve, and Sarah on a monthly basis for over two years. These studies of children have examined productive

3

(speaking) and receptive (listening) language, and the findings are generally reported in terms of the child's phonological, syntactic, or semantic growth.

Cognitive psychologists study child language for similar reasons, although they are primarily interested in what inferences can be made about cognitive or intellectual development. For this reason, cognitive psychologists are interested in the child's semantic knowledge since it may provide insights into the child's conceptual development. Most notable among the studies of cognitive development and language is the work done by Piaget (1970) during the forty-five year period between 1935 and 1980. A thorough review of the work in this area is provided by Clark and Clark (1977).

Other researchers in the disciplines of child development, psychology, linguistics, and education study child language because they hope to provide classroom teachers with information about how reading and language arts instruction should be conducted. Among such investigations are those conducted by Strickland (1962) and Rush, Moe, and Manning (1979) who compared child language to the written language children encounter in learning to read. Loban's (1963, 1976) longitudinal study of children from kindergarten through grade twelve represents the most extensive investigation of the language learning and language development of school-age students.

Other investigators (Martin et al., 1976; Hart, Walker, and Gray, 1977) have provided insights into the relationship between the oral language of children and the nature of literacy education achieved by children. Most investigators of child language believe that studies of the language used by children at the *lower levels of instruction* can provide core or essential vocabularies for elementary school instruction.

VOCABULARY DIVERSITY

The diversity of a child's speaking vocabulary is determined by the stock of words in the child's internal lexicon. The child with a limited vocabulary will exhibit little diversity, whereas the child with an extensive vocabulary will exhibit, or has the ability to exhibit, much greater diversity.

Vocabulary diversity may be examined by comparing samples of language from individual children. If the language sample is limited to a specified number of total words (tokens) such as 500, for example, and the child speaks 400 different words (types) in uttering the 500 words, the child demonstrates much vocabulary richness. However, if a child utters 500 total words with only 50 different words used, little diversity is demonstrated.[1]

The authors have employed vocabulary diversity measures in five of their studies (Hopkins, 1977, 1978; Moe, 1974; Moe and Hopkins, 1975; Rush,

---

[1] The ratio is determined by dividing the number of different words (the types) by the number of total words used (the tokens). In the first example, (400 ÷ 500) the ratio is .8. In the second example, (50 ÷ 500) the ratio is .1.

1980; Rush, Moe, and Manning, 1979). When comparing two or more groups of children the type-token ratio was utilized (Carroll, 1939, 1964). The collective studies appear to warrant a single conclusion concerning the vocabulary richness of first-grade children. As *individuals,* most first-grade children have extensive speaking vocabularies, and *as a group,* first-grade children have an extremely extensive speaking vocabulary.

ANALYZING LANGUAGE WITH COMPUTERS

During the early 1970s, Moe experimented with several computer programs that were developed for analyzing text.[2] After several changes, programs were developed that would take text, that is, connected words in sentences and connected sentences in paragraphs, as input data and provide a printout with a list or lists of the words that made up the analyzed text. Specific information on the various computer programs used by the authors has been reported elsewhere (Moe, 1980).

Early uses of computers for language study were restricted to analyses of the written materials used in the introductory stages of reading instruction. One study (Moe, 1973) provided a list of the high-frequency words found in the picture books often used with primary-level students.

Later uses of computer programs by the authors have provided additional information such as syllable counts, readability estimates, and type-token ratios, but in all cases, the program feature of providing lists of the words used in the text examined has been retained.

The major advantage of using computers for language analysis, however, is that enormous amount of text — hundreds of thousands of words — may be analyzed in a short period of time. At present, there are computers capable of performing up to 400 million calculations *in a second.* Furthermore, with the availability of low-cost microcomputers, it is now possible to conduct some language analyses in classrooms or even in homes.

ORGANIZATION OF THIS BOOK

Chapter II presents a review of previous word counts and words lists as they pertain to children's oral language.

Chapter III provides a brief review of oral language collection techniques including those used for the vocabulary presented in this volume. Information concerning the children sampled and the data analysis is presented, as is information concerning the length of the words the children spoke. Information regarding the cumulative frequencies of the most commonly used words is also presented in Chapter III.

---

[2]Language in written form is text. Hence, child oral language becomes text once it is transcribed.

Chapter IV provides information concerning the use of the oral vocabulary list in language arts education. Information concerning the relationship between the child's oral language performance and reading, writing, and spelling instruction is also included here.

Chapter V contains an alphabetical listing of all 6,412 words. Each word has its frequency of occurrence presented next to it.

Chapter VI presents a frequency listing of all 6,412 words in descending order of occurrence. Each word has its percentage of use listed next to it.

REFERENCES

Brown, R. *A First Language: Early Stages.* Cambridge, Massachusetts: Harvard University Press, 1973.

Carroll, J.B. Determining and numerating adjectives in children's speech. *Child Development, 10*:215-229, 1939.

Carroll, J.B. *Language and Thought.* Englewood Cliffs, New Jersey: Prentice-Hall, 1964.

Clark, H.H. and Clark, E.V. *Psychology and Language: An Introduction to Psycholinguistics.* New York: Harcourt, Brace, Jovanovich, 1977.

Hart, N.W.M., Walker, R.F. and Gray, B. *The Language of Children: A Key to Literacy.* Reading, Massachusetts: Addison-Wesley, 1977.

Hopkins, C.J. *The prediction of third-grade reading achievement from selected measures of first-grade oral language.* Paper presented at the annual meeting of the National Reading Conference, New Orleans, 1977.

Hopkins, C.J. The prediction of third-grade reading achievement from selected measures of first-grade oral language. *Resources in Education, 13*:49, 1978.

Loban, W.D. *The Language of Elementary School Children.* Champaign, Illinois: National Council of Teachers of English, 1963.

Loban, W.D. *Language Development: Kindergarten Through Grade Twelve.* Champaign, Illinois: National Council of Teachers of English, 1976.

Martin, N., Williams, P., Wilding, J., Hemmings, S. and Medway, P. *Understanding Children Talking.* Baltimore: Penguin Books, 1976.

McCarthy, D.A. The language development of the preschool child. *Institute of Child Welfare Monograph Series,* No. 4, 1930.

Menyuk, P. *Sentences Children Use.* Cambridge, Massachusetts: M.I.T. Press, 1969.

Moe, A.J. Words lists for beginning readers. *Reading Improvement, 10*:11-15, 1973.

Moe, A.J. *A comparative study of vocabulary diversity: The speaking vocabularies of first-grade children, the vocabularies of selected first-grade primers, and the vocabularies of selected first-grade trade books.* Paper presented at the annual meeting of the American Educational Research Association, Chicago, 1974.

Moe, A.J. Analyzing text with computers. *Education Technology, 20*:29-31, 1980.

Moe, A.J. and Hopkins, C.J. *The speaking vocabularies of kindergarten, first-grade and second-grade children.* Paper presented at the annual meeting of the National Conference on Research in English, Washington, D.C., 1975. Abstract in *Resources in Education, 10*:64, 1975.

Piaget, J. Piaget's theory. In Mussen, P.H. (Ed.): *Charmichael's Manual of Child Psychology*, Vol. 1, Third Edition. New York: John Wiley & Sons, 1970.

Rush, R.T. *The Prediction of End-of-Year Reading Achievement Through Case Grammar Constructs Found in the Spoken Discourse of Beginning First-Grade Children.* Unpublished doctoral dissertation, Purdue University, 1980.

Rush, R.T., Moe, A.J. and Manning, J.C. A comparison of basal reader language and the oral language of beginning first-grade children. *Journal of Educational Research, 73*: 12-15, 1979.

Strickland, R.G. The language of elementary school children: Its relationship to the language of reading textbooks and the quality of reading of selected children. *Bulletin of the College of Education*, 38. Bloomington, Indiana: Indiana University, 1962.

Templin, M.C. Certain language skills in children: Their development and interrelationships. *Institute of Child Welfare Monograph Series*, No. 26. Minneapolis: University of Minnesota Press, 1957.

Chapter II

A HISTORY OF WORD COUNTS AND WORD LISTS OF CHILDREN'S ORAL LANGUAGE

THE desire to document children's oral vocabularies is not a new interest nor is it restricted to educators and researchers. Many parents document early words in their children's baby books, in telephone calls to grandparents, and in comparisons of their child's language development with that of the child next door. In fact, prior to late 1920s and early 1930s, most of the early oral language investigations were biographical studies conducted by parents concerned with vocabulary acquisition. Termed "baby biographies," these studies were approached through a diary method.

In 1909, the Whipples, parents of a three-year-old boy, recorded each word that they heard their son use in sentences for ten days prior to his third birthday. Mr. and Mrs. Bush (1914) recorded all of the words that they heard their daughter use from age two and one-half until her third birthday and then made comparisons of the 1,944 different words she used with the 1,771 different words used by the Whipple's son. Similar studies were conducted by Brandenburg (1915) and Nice (1915), who analyzed the vocabulary words in their own children's speech, Langenbeck (1915), who listed the words used by a child described as "unusually precocious," and Stern (1924) who gathered data about the language of his own three children by reading his wife's diary. Researchers in favor of formal testing and carefully controlled investigations voiced criticism of these early studies, claiming that the biographical approach lacked systematic data gathering techniques and reflected inadequate sampling procedures.

Subsequent research turned to vocabulary analyses based on a larger number of children. Horn (1925) identified the most common words in the oral vocabulary of children through age six by combining the words obtained from three unpublished investigations. The first of these studies combined the spoken vocabularies of eighty children spanning an age range of one to six years. Two hundred thousand running words of the spoken vocabulary of kindergarten children in Iowa and Minnesota were analyzed for the second investigation. Horn's third set of data was the seventy thousand running

8

words Packer (1921) collected for an analysis of the oral vocabulary of first-grade children in Detroit, obtained by recording words children said in connection with school activities. The combined results of these three studies yielded approximately five thousand different words, which were then condensed to a list of 1,084 different words.

Gates (1926, 1935) compiled a reading vocabulary for the primary grades, which included the words from Horn's (1925) study as well as the 2,500 words of highest frequency published in Thorndike's (1921) word book for teachers. Other unpublished studies containing lists of words that children knew and used before entering first grade were summarized in the 1928 International Kindergarten Union study. This study contained a list of 2,596 words that occurred most frequently of the seven thousand different words reported. Dolch (1936) then chose the 510 words occurring one hundred times or more on the International Kindergarten Union list and included them as part of the data base for the popular Dolch list.

After a twenty-year lapse in which virtually no oral language vocabulary studies appeared in the literature, results of the most extensive oral vocabulary study ever conducted were published by Murphy in 1957. She summarized 1,195,098 running words obtained from several group studies based on conversations of 350 to 400 middle-class students in kindergarten through grade three living in Boston and Georgia.

Wepman and Hass (1969) demonstrated renewed interest in vocabulary study as they analyzed the oral responses of thirty five-, six-, and seven-year-old middle class children viewing the picture cards of the Thematic Apperception Test. While these words were coded by grammatical classification into the thirteen parts of speech, no information was reported as to the total number of words elicited or the number of different words analyzed.

The Basic Sight Vocabulary List was developed by Johnson (1971) by combining words from first-grade children's spontaneous speaking vocabulary on Murphy's (1957) list and the five hundred most frequently occurring words in the Kucera-Francis (1967) study of adult printed materials.

Sherk (1973) analyzed 121,391 words used by eighty black disadvantaged children in Kansas City Headstart programs, kindergarten, and first-grade as they responded to a series of pictures. Sherk reported that 5,080 different words were used, although it is somewhat difficult to compare this total with that of other lists since mispronunciations of words, dialect variations, and words with omitted endings were counted as separate words. Traditionally, words included in vocabulary studies have been recorded in conventional orthography.

Other word counts of oral vocabulary have been conducted by Hopkins, Moe, and Stephens (1975) and Moe and Hopkins (1975), who reported on the speaking vocabularies of kindergarten, first-grade, and second-grade children from middle socioeconomic status neighborhoods. Using standardized language elicitation procedures, these researchers demonstrated that it was possible to collect substantial samples of natural language that could be used to examine the vocabulary diversity of primary-grade children.

Hart, Walker, and Gray (1977) collected 93 samples of two and one-half to six and one-half year old Australian children's language and analyzed them to discover what single words, two-word, and three-word sequences were used at each age level and how and with what intended meaning they were combined. By multiplying the raw frequency of use by the percentage of the total sample of children who used the word or sequence, an adjusted index of use, called the communication index, was developed by these researchers. The purpose of this adjustment was to reflect the generality of the usage rather than the degree of repetition, which might be peculiar to one or two children.

The most recent study of children's oral vocabulary reported in the literature was conducted by Hopkins (1979) who identified the high-frequency words in the spontaneous oral vocabulary of 125 first-grade children from a sample of more than one hundred thousand running words.

From the review of research focusing on children's oral vocabulary, one can see that, with the exception of some of the studies conducted over the past several years, oral vocabulary studies have been quite interrelated. Many lists have been derived from combinations of data from previously published or unpublished research or both. Some investigators have failed to report the number of subjects used and the criteria for selection. In few studies have the procedures used to elicit the samples of language been described in enough detail to permit replication. While several lists include samples of the language of first-grade children, seldom has the language of more than twenty or thirty children been sampled.

REFERENCES

Brandenburg, G.C. The language of a three-year-old child. *Pedagogical Seminary, 22*: 89-120, 1915.

Bush, A.D. The vocabulary of a three-year-old girl. *Pedagogical Seminary, 21*:125-142, 1914.

Child Study Committee of the International Kindergarten Union. *A Study of the Vocabulary of Children Before Entering the First Grade.* Baltimore, Maryland: The International Kindergarten Union, 1928.

Dolch, E.W. A basic sight vocabulary. *Elementary School Journal, 36*:450-460, 1936.

Gates, A.I. *A Reading Vocabulary for the Primary Grades.* New York, New York: Bureau of Publications, Teachers College, Columbia University, 1926.

Gates, A.I. *A Reading Vocabulary for the Primary Grades.* Revised and Enlarged. New York, New York: Bureau of Publications, Teachers College, Columbia University, 1935.

Hart, N.W.M., Walker, R.F. and Gray, B. *The Language of Children: A Key to Literacy.* Reading, Massachusetts: Addison-Wesley Publishing Company, 1977.

Hopkins, C.J. The spontaneous oral vocabulary of children in grade one. *Elementary School Journal,* 79:240-249, 1979.

Hopkins, C.J., Moe, A.J. and Stephens, M.I. *A comparison of four oral language elicitation probes used with kindergarten, first-, and second-grade children.* Paper presented at the annual meeting of the Midwest Association for the Education of Young Children, Madison, Wisconsin, 1975.

Horn, E. Appropriate materials for instruction in reading. In Report of the National Committee on Reading, Whipple, G.M. (Ed.). *Twenty-Fourth Yearbook of the National Society for the Study of Education, Part I.* Bloomington, Illinois: Public School Publishing Company, 1925.

Johnson, D.D. A basic vocabulary for beginning reading. *Elementary School Journal,* 72:29-34, 1971.

Kucera, H. and Francis, W.N. *Computational Analysis of Present-Day American English.* Providence, Rhode Island: Brown University Press, 1967.

Langenbeck, M. A study of a five-year-old child. *Pedagogical Seminary, 22:*65-88, 1915.

Moe, A.J. and Hopkins, C.J. *The speaking vocabularies of kindergarten, first-grade and second-grade children.* Paper presented at the annual meeting of the National Conference on Research in English, Washington, D.C., before 1975.

Murphy, H. The spontaneous speaking vocabulary of children in primary grades. *Journal of Education, 140:*3-106, 1957.

Nice, N.M. The development of a child's vocabulary in relation to environment. *Pedagogical Seminary, 22:*35-64, 1915.

Packer, J.L. The vocabularies of ten first readers. In Report of the Society's Committee on Silent Reading, Whipple, G.M. (Ed.) *Twentieth Yearbook of the National Society for the Study of Education, Part II.* Bloomington, Illinois: Public School Publishing Company, 1921.

Sherk, J.K. *A Word-Count of Spoken English of Culturally Disadvantaged Preschool and Elementary Pupils.* Kansas City, Missouri: University of Missouri, 1973.

Stern, W. *Psychology of Early Childhood up to the Sixth Year of Age.* New York: Holt, 1924.

Thorndike, E.L. *The Teacher's Word Book.* New York, New York: Bureau of Publications, Teacher's College, Columbia University, 1921.

Wepman, J.M. and Hass, W. *A Spoken Word Count (Children — ages 5, 6 and 7).* Chicago: Language Research Associates, 1969.

Whipple, G.M., and Whipple, (Mrs.) G.M. The vocabulary of a three-year-old boy with some interpretive comments. *Pedagogical Seminary, 16:*1-22, 1909.

Chapter III

COLLECTION AND ANALYSIS
OF CHILDREN'S ORAL LANGUAGE

RESEARCH concerning the oral language of children is based on the assumption that the oral language studied represents that of children in general. The oral language of children is affected by the characteristics of the children and the conditions under which it is produced. Attention of researchers has, therefore, focused on selection of subjects who are typical of children at their age or grade level. Researchers have also attempted to identify settings and procedures that yield valid and reliable oral language samples.

Smith (1926) studied the language development of 273 children, eight months to six years of age, examining their vocabulary development. Smith's use of a large sample of subjects increased the likelihood that the language sampled validly represented the language of children in general. Her examination of "spontaneous chatter," however, made it difficult to replicate her study and, thus, to determine if the children's language was representative.

McCarthy (1930) conducted a study of the language development of twenty children at six month age intervals from eighteen to fifty-four months. To insure that her sample validly represented the population of children as a whole, McCarthy used sampling procedures believed to assure a balanced distribution of socioeconomic factors, intelligence, and sex. McCarthy employed an adult-child interview, which involved the use of a set of toys to stimulate children's oral language. The process yielded a sample of each child's language in which the child's language performance was thought to reflect his or her competence. In other words, children were thought to use their best syntax and vocabulary when interviewed by adults. McCarthy's methods were widely employed in research until at least 1960.

Criticism of oral language data collection procedures as structured by McCarthy have focused on the likelihood that variations in the stimulus materials and the conversational styles of the adult interviewers induce variations in the responses of the children being interviewed. That is, unless the interview process is controlled, the language produced might be a distorted representation of the language of the child and, thus, of the group of children typified by the child. In presenting these criticisms, Longhurst and Grubb (1974) concluded that the best method of collecting a sample of a child's oral language was an adult-child interview in which the interviewer questioned the child on a variety of topics.

A method of collecting samples of child language was designed and field tested by Hopkins, Moe, and Stephens (1975) in response to the criticism of the child-adult interview process. Their intent was to devise a set of oral language elicitation probes that would (1) obtain large amounts of oral language from children, (2) require little time to administer, (3) require no test materials except a tape recorder, and (4) require no specialized training to administer. Their oral language data collection procedure is detailed in the Data Collection section of this chapter. It was this procedure that was used to obtain the oral language forming the data base for *The Vocabulary of First-Grade Children.*

THE CHILDREN

Several studies of the spoken discourse of first-grade children contributed to the vocabulary data presented in this volume. Of the 329 children whose spoken language contributed to the total project, 300 participated in studies designed to investigate the relationship between language development and reading achievement in grade one. Each of these children was randomly selected from the population of all first graders in five north-central Indiana communities with populations ranging from 25,000 to 45,000. The children were representative of the full range of socioeconomic levels in their communities. Of the remaining children who contributed oral language samples, twenty-five were selected because they were enrolled in a school where high levels of language and academic skills were the norm. The balance of the children whose language contributed to *The Vocabulary of First-Grade Children* were selected because they were believed to be typical first graders.

Among the 329 children, there was an approximately equal distribution of girls and boys. All of the children spoke English as their first and only language. Fifteen of the children were Black; the remainder were Caucasian. Their ages ranged from five years and ten months to eight years and four months. The mean age at the time of data collection was six years and nine months.

DATA COLLECTION

In order to obtain samples of spoken discourse, a structured interview was held with each of the children who participated in the studies conducted by the authors. The interviews varied in duration from twelve to twenty-five minutes according to the nature of the specific study of which they were a part. The average number of words spoken during the interviews was 870. In total, the 329 children interviewed produced a corpus of 286,108 words containing, 6,412 different words.[1]

Each child was interviewed privately, in quiet, familiar surroundings such as an unused schoolroom or the school nurse's office. Each interviewer was skilled in work with young children and familiar to the children in the school where the interview took place.

A routine was followed by the interviewer that was designed to put the child at ease and to elicit a large amount of spoken discourse in a short period of time. The interviewer went to the child's classroom and asked the child to accompany him or her to a familiar room where they could talk. On the way to the interview room, the child was engaged in casual conversation about topics unrelated to the interview in order to allay anxiety and to establish rapport.

In the interview room, the child and the interviewer were seated on chairs at adjoining sides of a small, children's-sized table on which an audio cassette tape recorder had been placed. The tape recorder was immediately set in the record mode where it remained until the interview was concluded.

The spoken discourse recorded during each interview was elicited by four probes that had been specifically developed by Hopkins, Moe, and Stephens (1975) for use in stimulating spoken responses from children. The four elicitation probes are as follows:

(1) "Tell me about your favorite game." The child was asked to explain how the game was played and to tell why it was his or her favorite.

(2) "Tell me about your favorite television show." The child was encouraged to tell why the program was his or her favorite and to relate an episode he or she remembered watching.

(3) "Tell me about the best thing or the most exciting thing that ever happened to you." The child was encouraged to relate a vivid personal experience.

(4) "Tell me a story." The child was told that the story could be one that he or she had heard or read before or one that was made up.

With four elicitation probes as its basis, each interview was conducted in a conversational manner. When the interviewer observed anxiety, as reflected by physical tenseness, extreme restlessness, or reticence, the interviewer moved so as to increase the physical distance between himself or herself and the child. When the child was talking comfortably, the inter-

---

[1] The deletion of onomatopoeia such as "buzz," "hiss," "whoosh," and "zoom" together with non-meaningful utterances such as "ah," "er," and "em" resulted in the deletion of 361 words. Thus, the total number of running words analyzed was 285, 747.

viewer leaned forward slightly in an expression of interest and, at appropriate intervals, expressed interest verbally with statements such as "Good, tell me more," "That's interesting, tell me more about that," or "What else can you tell me about that?" On occasions when the child seemed unable or unwilling to respond further, the interviewer's response was of this nature: "Okay, that's fine, now tell me about. . ." or, if all four elicitation probes had been presented, "Okay, fine, now would you like to listen to some of what we have talked about?" Under no circumstances was a child required to initiate or continue participation in an interview against his or her wishes.

About one-tenth of the 286,108 running word oral language sample that forms the data base for this book was obtained by recording the spontaneous language produced by children at play. These individual samples were obtained through the use of a microcassette recorder equipped with a lapel microphone. The recorder was placed in a bicyclist's around-the-waist backpack and worn by individual children who had been previously interviewed. The settings in which spontaneous oral language was recorded were playgrounds or classrooms during recess or free play periods during the school day.

Children were oriented to the equipment by Rush who demonstrated its use and the manner in which it was to be worn to all children in each classroom cooperating in the study. The children typically viewed the recorder as a sign of prestige, with only one child in eighty-five refusing to wear it.

The use of the microcassette recorder, which was managed by classroom teachers after ten-minute orientation sessions, enabled the collection of spontaneous oral language samples without the use of complex remote recording equipment.

DATA ANALYSIS

Preparation of spoken discourse recordings for computer analysis required that each recording be transcribed and keypunched. All statements made by the child, whether spontaneous or in response to an interview probe or question, were considered to be part of the language sample. A series of rules was adopted in order to establish sentence boundaries and word spellings.

Sentence and utterance conventions were largely based on those used by Strickland (1962) and were adhered to in transcribing recorded spoken discourse. With respect for the oral language characteristics of each child, the following rules were observed:

(1) Period punctuation was used to terminate the sentence or utterance when voice pitch fell distinctly at the end of a series of words.

(2) Rising pitch at the end of an interrogatory sentence or utterance signalled punctuation with a question mark.

(3) Sentence or utterance intonation and stress with signalled exclamation were used as cues for exclamation point punctuation.

(4) In cases where the child started a sentence or utterance, stopped, and restarted the sentence or utterance, the false start was followed by two hyphens and a space followed by the reworded sentence or utterance.

In preparing transcripts of the children's spoken discourse, the following word-related conventions were applied:

(1) Hyphenated words such as *loop-the-loop* and *first-grade,* were counted as single words.

(2) Compound words were counted as one word (e.g. *kickball* was counted as one word).

(3) Inflected forms of words were counted as separate words (e.g. *captured* was counted as distinct from its root, *capture*).

(4) Contractions such as *can't* and *don't* were counted as distinct from *cannot* and *do not.*

(5) Numbers were recorded in words, rather than numeral form (e.g. *twenty-five* was transcribed instead of *25*).

(6) Some single letters were recorded as words (e.g. in "He got a B and I got an A," *B* and *A* were transcribed and counted as words.

(7) Expressions such as *"uh-huh," "uh-uh," "um,"* and *"huh"* were not counted as words, and thus do not occur in the word lists presented in this book.

(8) In general, American slang words produced in the interview setting by the children were transcribed verbatim.

(9) In cases where the quality of the recorded transcript occasionally rendered a word unintelligible, after three attempts to discriminate it, the transcriber inserted a word that fit the phonetic, syntactic, and semantic context of the child's utterance.

(10) Dialectal variations and omitted vowels, consonants, and word endings were transcribed in conventional orthography. Thus, words such as *gonna* were recorded as *going to*.

(11) Neologisms, that is, words invented or coined by the children, were included in the transcripts. Many of these were verb tenses such as *swammed, tooken, shutted,* and *stabbeded* or adjectives like *twicest* and *swolled.*

The computer program used to analyze the language samples produces an output, which is checked through the use of a separate spelling dictionary program. Words occurring on the printout but not in the computer dictionary were checked by the authors. If they could be verified, they were kept as part of the sample. Otherwise, these unusual words were either corrected or deleted.

Subsequent to the transcription and keypunching of all 329 spoken discourse samples, the individual samples were concatenated to form one continuous stream of sentences and utterances 286,108 words in length. This corpus of transcribed spoken discourse formed the basis of the vocabulary list presented here.

The computer program employed in the analysis of the spoken discourse sample has been used in several studies of children's language development (McDaniel and Moe, 1973; Hopkins, 1979; Rush and Moe, 1977; Rush, 1980). Information about a number of syntactic and semantic factors is available in the output of the program. Output information utilized in developing *The Vocabulary of First-Grade Children* included the following:

(1)   the total number of words in the sample
(2)   the number of different words in the sample
(3)   an alphabetized listing of all different words
(4)   a frequency of use figure for each word
(5)   a listing of words based on frequency of use
(6)   a percentage of use figure for each word

Information about other vocabulary-related factors is available in the output of the computer programs. For example, the language sample may be analyzed according to the number of times each length word is used. Results of word-length analyses for *The Vocabulary of First-Grade Children* indicate that:

1 letter words were used 14,937 times
2 letter words were used 47,121 times
3 letter words were used 81,344 times
4 letter words were used 69,496 times
5 letter words were used 31,968 times
6 letter words were used 19,000 times
7 letter words were used 12,249 times
8 letter words were used 5,554 times
9 letter words were used 2,554 times
10 letter words were used 1,117 times
11 letter words were used   258 times
12 letter words were used   120 times
13 letter words were used   11 times

14 letter words were used	8 times
15 letter words were used	8 times
16 letter words were used	2 times
17 or more letter words were used	0 times

The average word length was 3.8 letters with a standard deviation of 1.7 letters.

Another interesting analysis is to examine the cumulative frequencies of words on the vocabulary list. In this corpus,

25 words account for 41.30 percent of the total words spoken
50 words account for 53.15 percent of the total words spoken
75 words account for 60.05 percent of the total words spoken
100 words account for 64.53 percent of the total words spoken
200 words account for 74.48 percent of the total words spoken
300 words account for 79.59 percent of the total words spoken
400 words account for 83.02 percent of the total words spoken
500 words account for 85.50 percent of the total words spoken
600 words account for 87.35 percent of the total words spoken
700 words account for 88.83 percent of the total words spoken
800 words account for 90.05 percent of the total words spoken
900 words account for 91.02 percent of the total words spoken
1000 words account for 91.84 percent of the total words spoken

The frequencies of 500 words on the list result in a large percentage of the words spoken. By the time the 500 most frequently used words have been identified, 85.5 percent of the total words spoken have been accounted for. A plateau is then reached, and at this point, the addition of the remaining 5,912 words on the list accounts for only 14.5 percent of the total corpus of words spoken.

PECULIAR WORDS

In the course of transcribing, keypunching, analyzing, and editing the oral language samples, the authors agreed upon spellings of terms for which no standard form seemed to have been previously specified. Indeed, some of the "words" used by the children and included in the word lists of Chapter VI, though they conveyed meaning, do not appear in dictionaries of standard American English. For example, *uh-huh* and *uh-uh* were used almost uniformly by the first-grade children to express *yes* and *no* answers respectively.

Other peculiar words used by the children can be classified as terms that result from the overgeneralization of standard English grammatical forms, colloquialisms, invented words, and partially or faultily learned words. Words such as *bestest, wonned, builded, meanestest,* and *stealed* are examples of overgeneralization of rules governing uses of inflected forms, a phenomenon that commonly occurs in the language of first graders. Examples of contexts in which such words were used are presented below:

> It's about some guy fighting dragons. The guy came to our school, he's going to fight the dragon. That's the guy that wouldn't talk. Guess who I like the *bestest*? The queen.

> We only have one more game to go. We *wonned* every one so far but one and we have to play the first ones again.

> We got thirteen of them. It took us a long time. *Builded* them. Uh, you take off some parts and you glue it together.

> They're the meanest ones. My cousins. They're the *meanestest*.

> So Popeye comes and says, "What's wrong Olive and Sweet Pea?" And Olive says, "Brutus *stealed* my hamburger and Brutus *stealed* my swing."

Colloquialisms, the second group of peculiar words, include terms such as *gots, throwed, hisself, somewheres,* and *spelt*. Words such as these were used by the children and seem representative of usage in their language communities. Some contextual excerpts of colloquial word usage are listed below:

> Cookie and Bozo, they're both clowns, they're both boys, you know. And Cookie, he's so funny he always *gots* to cook you know.

> Yesterday I saw it, yesterday Cookie *throwed* the icing at *hisself*.

> After you have *finded* who is going to be it and hide their eyes you take and you hide somewhere *like* maybe in a closet or *somewheres*.

> I know about Tonya. I *spelt* it. I'm putting it. I'm gonna keep it on this one.

A third group of unusual words is comprised of words that the children seemed to make up out of need. These words were quite puzzling to observe in the word lists and were at first assumed to be typographical or keypunching errors. However, when the contexts in which such words occurred were parsed out of the larger corpus of language for closer inspection, the word meanings became clear. The following selections of oral language illustrate how some of the children modified and combined existing words in order to express the meaning they had in mind.

> Operation. There's this man. And there's a whole bunch of bones like. And then you have these *pleezers* like. And you try to take them and without making him buzz.

> And started his car and backed it out and then ran over him and broke his hand. *Sprunged* his wrist.

Salt and ice water. That hurt, too. I couldn't put my foot in it. They had hot water on it. It had a big — My ankle was *swolled* up out to here. I couldn't even wear my shoes.

... to mash the potatoes — and he mashed them with one of those things you use the cement for. I didn't get to taste them. They must have tasted *cementy*.

A fourth group of peculiar words is comprised of those terms that were obviously used in place of a real word and that represented a partial or faulty learning of the correct word. Examples, in context, of such terms follow:

We went to the zoo before. It had mouses and all those stuff. And bears and snakes. And monkeys. And Flipper too. And gorillas, *chimfanzines*.

When Scott my little brother was born. He is one now and his birthday is on January twenty-seventh. Well I got my last. It is a *deskstar* space station.

Clearly, it might be argued that some, if not all, of the words deemed "peculiar" by the authors are not words at all, in the strictest sense. The children, however, did use such terms to express meaning that could be ascertained through the context of their oral language. Because meaning was expressed, such terms were counted as words and included in the word lists. An asterisk is used to distinguish them from words that are accepted as true, if less colorful, English words.

REFERENCES

Hart, N.W.M., Walker, R.F. and Gray, B. *The Language of Children: A Key to Literacy.* Reading, Massachusetts: Addison-Wesley, 1977.

Hopkins, C.J. The spontaneous oral vocabulary of children in grade one. *Elementary School Journal,* 79:240-249, 1979.

Hopkins, C.J., Moe, A.J. and Stephens, M.I. *A comparison of four oral language elicitation probes used with kindergarten, first-, and second-grade children.* Paper presented at the annual meeting of the Midwest Association for the Education of Young Children, Madison, Wisconsin, 1975.

Longhurst, T.M. and Grubb, S. A comparison of language samples collected in four situations. *Language Speech and Hearing Services in Schools,* 5:71-78, 1974.

McCarthy, D.A. The language development of the preschool child. *Institute for Child Welfare Monograph Series,* No. 4, 1930.

McDaniel, E. and Moe, A.J. High-frequency words used in the writing of second-grade students from varying socioeconomic and ethnic backgrounds. *Education,* 93:241-245, 1973.

Rush, R.T. *The Prediction of End-of-Year Reading Achievement Through Case-Grammar Constructs Found in the Spoken Discourse of Beginning First-Grade Children.* Unpublished doctoral dissertation, Purdue University, 1980.

Rush, R.T. and Moe, A.J. *The correspondence between syntactical features of primary basal reader language and the oral language of beginning first-grade children.* Paper presented at the annual meeting of the National Reading Conference, New Orleans, 1977.

Smith, M.E. An investigation of the development of the sentence and extent of vocabulary in young children. *University of Iowa Studies in Child Welfare.* Iowa City: University of Iowa, 1926.

Strickland, R. The language of elementary school children: Its relationship to the language of reading textbooks and the quality of reading of selected children. *Bulletin of the School of Education of Indiana University, 38,* 1962.

Chapter IV

USE OF ORAL VOCABULARY LISTS
IN LANGUAGE ARTS INSTRUCTION

B ECAUSE of the integrated nature of language arts instruction, a word list with a solid foundation in children's own oral language provides a useful base upon which other language activities may be planned.

ORAL LANGUAGE AND READING

The relationship between oral language fluency and reading achievement has been a relatively frequent topic of concern in the literature (Dahl, 1975, 1981; Fox, 1976; Hopkins, 1976, 1981; Groff, 1977; Rush, 1980). There is evidence that at about the kindergarten and first-grade levels, children achieve much oral language growth (Loban, 1963; O'Donnell, Griffin, and Norris, 1967; Fox, 1970). Most of the research concerning oral language and reading has been influenced by the prevailing grammatical theory at the time the study was conducted (Fox, 1970). Since the 1920s, four periods of research, sometimes overlapping, may be identified. They are as follows:

(1) 1925-1960. Studies conducted during the period in which investigators utilized traditional Latin-based grammar concepts.
(2) 1960-1970. Studies conducted by the researchers who were influenced by the structural grammar theorists.
(3) 1965-1975. Studies in which investigators applied transformational grammar concepts.
(4) 1975-present. Studies that utilized grammars such as those employed in discourse analysis, which went beyond sentences as the unit of measurement.

Evidence exists to indicate that there is some relationship between oral language development and reading achievement, particularly in the primary grades. The relationship, however, is not nearly as high as might be suspected. Studies in which researchers have attempted detailed analyses of children's oral language have failed to identify specific semantic or syntactic aspects of language that seem closely related to reading achievement. Investigators who have conducted such studies have often concluded that the lack of strong evidence in support of such a relationship may result from difficulties in eliciting, analyzing, and quantifying oral language data. It is possible that the methodological procedures developed by Fillmore (1968) and Kintsch (1974) and employed by Rush (1980) may provide some evidence of a higher relationship between oral language and reading when applied in longitudinal studies.

Regardless of the lack of strong empirical support for relating oral language ability to reading achievement, the fact remains that reading is a language-based skill. Children anticipate that written words will make sense or carry meaning just as spoken words do. Thus, children must learn to recognize printed words as being the written counterpart of those words they already know and use. To help children make the transition from speech to print, teachers may employ the language experience approach, a method that uses children's dictated accounts of daily experiences and activities as the source of instructional materials. Repeated encounters of high-frequency words help children develop their sight vocabularies as well as phonic skills, structural analysis skills, and facility in using context as a means of recognizing words. The high-frequency words on the oral vocabulary list presented in Chapter VI may be used by teachers to identify words used most often by children and thus likely to be repeated in their stories. These print forms of words may then be emphasized in the reading and discusion of language experience stories. It should be noted that there is a great deal of overlap between high-frequency words on the oral vocabulary list and lists of high-frequency words occurring in printed text.

Another related use of the oral vocabulary list for reading instruction is in the selection of words to be included in textbooks and tradebooks written for children. Authors may wish to consult such a list if they are concerned with including words that children understand and use at the time of beginning reading instruction.

The list could also be used to determine the familiarity of words that might be used on vocabulary subtests often included as part of reading achievement tests. Similarly, the list might be used as an aid in the selection of basic vocabularies to be taught to non-English speaking students learning our language.

ORAL LANGUAGE AND WRITING

It is frequently recommended that experiences in written communication begin early in grade one (Moffett, 1973; Sealey, Sealey, and Millmore, 1979; Petty and Jensen, 1980). As this book reveals, children begin first grade with a rich oral vocabulary. They often show interest in written language and attempt to write names and simple messages. Such acts indicate readiness for instruction in writing and spelling.

Because children are most likely to want to write about the things they talk about, an oral vocabulary list seems to have special applications in the first-grade writing program. Such a list might be used to determine the words children should learn to write or spell first. High-frequency words produced in oral language also occur with high frequency in written language. Thus, it makes good sense for teachers to be familiar with such words and to teach them as part of early writing experiences. The teaching of high-frequency words might also be integrated into routine classroom activities as teaching opportunities present themselves.

Another possible use of the high-frequency word list would be to arrange the words thematically according to topics familiar to the children. Lists developed in this way might then be provided to the children for reference during independent writing activities.

Using the high-frequency word list as a basic reference, teachers might expand the list in order to make it even more relevant to their pupils. This would require that the teachers observe sources of words that might have special utility for the children they teach. Television programs, field trips, and personal and shared experiences are examples of sources of words that might be considered common for any given group.

ORAL LANGUAGE AND SPELLING

In teaching children to spell, attention is often focused on letter patterns. Groups of words with similar patterns are presented to learners who might master several similarly spelled words more easily than words presented separately. Teachers might wish to select high-frequency words from the list in Chapter VI that correspond to the patterns introduced in their phonic pattern-based spelling programs.

Other current spelling programs are based on the research and writing of Ernest Horn, who for more than fifty years has advocated that spelling programs be based on word frequency. Horn (1971) recommends that spelling instruction be based on high-frequency words, which may or may not conform to phonic or orthographic generalizations.

Of the many lists that might be used as the basis for first-grade spelling programs (Horn, 1927; Fitzgerald, 1951), most are based on the written language of children and adults. Such lists seem valid for pupils whose writing skills approximate their oral language skills. In the first grade where the relationship between oral and written language is formally introduced, however, it seems more appropriate to teach the spelling of the words that first-grade children use in their speech. The oral language of first-graders includes the words they write, but it is not restricted to them. Thus, incorporating the oral vocabulary word list into the first-grade spelling program might enable more flexible and natural written communication. The use of such a vocabulary list in first-grade spelling and writing programs is consistent, moreover, with the belief that language instruction of all forms should be meaningful to the learner. Familiar words are more meaningful than words the learner has never encountered and are, therefore, easier to learn to read and write.

REFERENCES ON VOCABULARY INSTRUCTION

There are several books that provide excellent techniques and sample exercises for vocabulary instruction in language arts and reading. Some of them are listed below:

Dale, E., O'Rourke, J. and Bamman, H.A. *Techniques of Teaching Vocabulary.* Addison, Illinois: Field Educational Publications, Inc., 1971.

Deighton, L.C. *Vocabulary Development in the Classroom.* New York: Teachers College Press, Teachers College, Columbia University, 1959.

Heilman, A.W. and Holmes, E.A. *Smuggling Language into the Teaching of Reading.* Columbus: Charles E. Merrill Publishing Company, 1972.

Ives, J.P., Bursuk, L.Z., and Ives, S.A. *Word Identification Techniques.* Chicago: Rand McNally Publishing Company, 1979.

Johnson, D.D. and Pearson, P.D. *Teaching Reading Vocabulary.* New York: Holt, Rinehart and Winston, 1978.

Sealey, L., Sealey, N. and Millmore, M. *Children's Writing: An Approach for the Early Grades.* Newark, Delaware: International Reading Association, 1979.

Yawkey, T.D., Askov, E.N., Cartwright, C.A., Dupuis, M.M., Fairchild, S.H. and Yawkey, M.L. *Language Arts and the Young Child.* Itasca, Illinois: F.E. Peacock Publishers, Inc., 1981.

The Vocabulary of First-Grade Children presents an oral language-based list of words used by young children, a description of how it was developed, and suggestions for its use. It is hoped that this book will be a valuable resource to teachers, authors, and child language researchers involved in the education of young children.

RERERENCES

Dahl, S.S. *An Identification of Language Variables Related to Success in Beginning Reading.* Unpublished doctoral dissertation, University of Wisconsin, Madison, 1975.

Dahl, S. Oral language and its relationship to success in reading. In Froese, V. and Straw, S.B. (Eds.): *Research in the Language Arts: Language and Schooling.* Baltimore: University Park Press, 1981.

Fillmore, C.J. The case for case. In Bach, E. and Harms, R.T. (Eds.): *Universals in Linguistic Theory.* New York: Holt Rinehart and Winston, 1968.

Fitzgerald, J.A. *A Basic Life Spelling Vocabulary,* Milwaukee: Bruce Publishing Company, 1951.

Fox, S.E. *Syntactic Maturity and Vocabulary Diversity in the Oral Language of Kindergarten and Primary School Children.* Unpublished doctoral dissertation, Indiana University, 1970.

Fox, S.E. Assisting children's language development. *Reading Teacher, 29:*666-670, 1976.

Groff, P. Oral language and reading. *Reading World, 17:*71-75, 1977.

Hopkins, C.J. *An Investigation of the Relationship of Selected Oral Language Measures and First-Grade Reading Achievement.* Unpublished doctoral dissertation, Purdue University, 1976.

Hopkins, C.J. Evaluating children's oral language. In Froese, V. and Straw, S.B. (Eds.): *Research in the Language Arts: Language and Schooling:* Baltimore: University Park Press, 1981.

Horn, E. *The Basic Writing Vocabulary.* Iowa City: University of Iowa, 1927.

Horn, E. *Teaching Spelling: What Research Says to the Teacher.* Washington, D.C.: National Education Association Publications, 1971.

Kintsch, W. *The Representation of Meaning in Memory.* Hillsdale, New Jersey: Lawrence Erlbaum Associates, 1974.

Loban, W.D. *The Language of Elementary School Children.* Champaign, Illinois: National Council of Teachers of English, 1963.

Moffett, J. *A Student-Centered Language Arts Curriculum, Grades K-6: A Handbook for Teachers.* Boston: Houghton Mifflin, 1973.

O'Donnell, R.C., Griffin, W.J., and Norris, R.C. *Syntax of Kindergarten and Elementary School Children: A Transformational Analysis.* Champaign, Illinois: National Council of Teachers of English, 1967.

Petty, W.T. and Jensen, J.M. *Developing Children's Language.* Boston: Allyn and Bacon, 1980.

Rush, R.T. *The Prediction of End-of-Year Reading Achievement Through Case Grammar Constructs Found in the Spoken Discourse of Beginning First-Grade Children.* Unpublished doctoral dissertation, Purdue University, 1980.

Sealey, L., Sealey, N. and Millmore, M. *Children's Writing: An Approach for the Primary Grades.* Newark, Delaware: International Reading Association, 1979.

Chapter V

ALPHABETICAL LISTING OF THE VOCABULARY

THE 6,412 word vocabulary is contained in this chapter beginning with the word *a* and ending with the word *zoomed*. The actual frequency of each word is found next to the word. Thus, *a* was used 6,716 times, *aardvark* was used 6 times, *about* was used 706 times, etc.

Asterisks appearing next to some entries on the word lists indicate that the words are not grammatically correct or standard English words which one would expect to find in a dictionary. In most cases, these words represent invented words, overgeneralizations of verb tenses, or nonexistent pronouns, all of which are quite common in young children's language. A few asterisked words, notably *founded, lighted,* and *slug,* appear to be legitimate words. However, within the context of the language samples, these words, too, were incorrect verb tenses.

WORD	FREQ.	WORD	FREQ.
A	6716	AHEAD	28
AARDVARK	6	AID	2
ABC'S	7	AIM	2
ABLE	12	AIMED	1
ABOARD	2	AIN'T	112
ABOMINABLE	8	AIR	49
ABOUT	706	AIRCRAFT	2
ABOVE	4	AIRPLANE	28
ABRAHAM	2	AIRPLANES	19
ACCIDENT	7	AIRPORT	2
ACCIDENTAL	6	AISLE	2
ACCOMPLISH	1	AJAX	2
ACCOUNT	1	AL	2
ACES	1	ALARMS	1
ACHE	2	ALASKA	1
ACORNS	2	ALBERT	2
ACRES	2	ALFALFA	16
ACROBATERS*	1	ALFALFA'S	5
ACROBATS	5	ALICE	6
ACROSS	61	ALICIA	1
ACT	21	ALIKE	2
ACTED	4	ALIVE	14
ACTING	4	ALL	2210
ACTION	3	ALL'S	3
ACTIVITY	1	ALLAN	2
ACTS	11	ALLEY	5
ACTUALLY	2	ALLIGATOR	15
AD	1	ALLIGATORS	6
ADAM	3	ALLISON	5
ADAMS	2	ALLOWANCES	2
ADD	4	ALLOWED	11
ADDED	1	ALMOST	126
ADDING	1	ALONE	19
ADRIAN	10	ALONG	54
ADRIAN'S	1	ALPHABET	2
ADVENTURE	1	ALREADY	60
AFFAIR	1	ALSO	44
AFFORD	2	ALTOGETHER	1
AFGHAN	1	ALWAYS	261
AFRAID	18	AM	41
AFRICA	3	AMAZING	1
AFTER	285	AMBULANCE	14
AFTERNOON	15	AMERICA	8
AFTERNOONS	1	AMERICAN	2
AGAIN	263	AMMUNITION	1
AGAINST	27	AMUSEMENT	1
AGE	2	AMY	3
AGENTS	1	AN	172
AGGRAVATION	4	AND	19376
AGO	57	ANDREA	5

WORD	FREQ.	WORD	FREQ.
ANDY	18	AQUAMAN	3
ANGEL	3	AQUARIUM	1
ANGELA	7	AQUARIUS	1
ANGELS	19	ARCHERY	2
ANGIE	18	ARCHIE	3
ANGRY	3	ARCHIES	4
ANIMAL	30	ARE	415
ANIMALS	69	AREN'T	21
ANITA	1	ARGUED	1
ANKLE	6	ARGUMENT	2
ANN	15	ARK	1
ANN'S	1	ARKANSAS	4
ANNA	8	ARM	26
ANNETTE	5	ARM'S	1
ANNIE	2	ARMS	20
ANOTHER	275	ARMSTRONG	14
ANSWER	5	ARMSTRONG'S	2
ANSWERED	21	ARMY	10
ANSWERS	3	ARNOLD'S	4
ANT	9	AROUND	476
ANTELOPE	2	ARREST	2
ANTENNAS	1	ARRESTED	3
ANTHONY	1	ARRESTS	1
ANTIQUE	3	ARROW	7
ANTS	12	ARROWS	4
ANY	341	ART	5
ANYBODY	31	ARTIE	1
ANYBODY'S	2	ARTIST	3
ANYHOW	1	AS	162
ANYONE	10	ASHES	6
ANYTHING	169	ASK	47
ANYWAY	13	ASKED	57
ANYWAYS*	2	ASKING	11
ANYWHERE	5	ASKS	8
APACHE	7	ASLEEP	39
APART	13	ASLEEPS*	1
APARTMENT	18	ASSOCIATED	1
APARTMENTS	8	ASTRONAUT	2
APE	15	AT	860
APES	11	ATARI	2
APOLLO	2	ATARIS	1
APOLOGIZE	2	ATE	210
APOLOGIZED	1	ATLANTA	1
APPLE	36	ATTACHED	1
APPLE'S	4	ATTACK	3
APPLES	46	ATTACKED	1
APPLESAUCE	2	ATTACKS	3
APRIL	4	ATTENTION	1
APRON	1	ATTIC	7
AQUA	2	AUCTION	1

WORD	FREQ.	WORD	FREQ.
AUDIENCE	3	BALLOONS	6
AUNT	48	BALLS	41
AUNT'S	9	BAM	1
AUNTIE	1	BAMM	8
AUNTS	2	BANANA	16
AUSTIN	28	BANANAS	5
AUSTIN'S	4	BAND	2
AUTO	2	BANDAGE	4
AUTOBIOGRAPHY	1	BANDAGED	3
AUTOGRAPH	2	BANDAID	2
AUTUMN	1	BANDAIDS	4
AVENUE	5	BANDITS	1
AWAKE	5	BANG	7
AWAY	215	BANGED	1
AWFUL	5	BANGING	1
AWHILE	13	BANGS	1
AX	2	BANK	28
B	14	BANKER	1
BAA	4	BANKS	3
BABIES	31	BAPTIZED	3
BABY	444	BAR	17
BABY'S	70	BARBARA	2
BABYSITTED*	1	BARBECUE	4
BABYSITTER	6	BARBER	1
BABYSITTING	1	BARBIE	4
BACK	785	BARBIE'S	2
BACKED	2	BARBIES	7
BACKPACK	1	BARE	1
BACKS	2	BAREFOOT	1
BACKWARD	1	BAREFOOTED	2
BACKWARDS	24	BARELY	3
BACON	7	BARETTA	9
BAD	137	BARGAIN	1
BADDER*	2	BARK	3
BADDEST*	3	BARKING	6
BADGE	3	BARKS	3
BADLANDS	1	BARN	21
BAG	37	BARNABY	1
BAGGIE	1	BARNACLE	4
BAGS	3	BARNEY	16
BAIT	3	BARNYARD	1
BAKE	5	BARON	1
BAKED	4	BARREL	13
BAKER	2	BARRELS	1
BAKERY	2	BARREN	1
BALANCE	3	BARRETTE	4
BALL	290	BARRETTES	3
BALLENGER	2	BARRY	1
BALLETS	1	BARS	22
BALLOON	4	BASE	75

WORD	FREQ.	WORD	FREQ.
BASEBALL	109	BEAST	1
BASEBALL'S	1	BEASTIE	2
BASEMENT	23	BEAT	41
BASES	22	BEATED*	3
BASKET	23	BEATEN	1
BASKETBALL	61	BEATING	3
BASKETS	7	BEATS	9
BASKIN	1	BEAUTIFUL	4
BASS	1	BEAUTY	1
BAT	78	BEAVER	5
BATGIRL	3	BEAVERS	1
BATH	4	BEAZLEY	1
BATHING	3	BECAME	2
BATHROOM	20	BECAUSE	1017
BATHROOMS	1	BECKY	4
BATHS	1	BED	391
BATHTUB	5	BED'S	1
BATMAN	46	BEDROOM	38
BATMOBILE	3	BEDROOMS	5
BATON	1	BEDS	23
BATS	12	BEDTIME	1
BATTED	1	BEE	18
BATTER	11	BEEF	2
BATTERIES	7	BEEHIVE	1
BATTERS	1	BEEHIVES	1
BATTERY	1	BEEN	423
BATTING	3	BEEP	17
BATTLE	3	BEEPS	2
BATTLESHIP	9	BEER	7
BATTLESTAR	6	BEES	11
BATTLING	4	BEESWAX	1
BAWLING	1	BEETLES	3
BAY	3	BEFORE	191
BB	3	BEG	2
BBS	2	BEGAN	1
BE	384	BEGGED	1
BEA	4	BEGGING	3
BEA'S	1	BEGIN	1
BEACH	19	BEGINNING	11
BEADS	1	BEGINS	2
BEAGLE	2	BEHAVE	3
BEAK	1	BEHIND	52
BEAM	2	BEHINDS	1
BEAN	4	BEIGE	1
BEANS	19	BEING	12
BEANSTALK	10	BEINGS	1
BEAR	520	BELCHER*	1
BEAR'S	183	BELIEVE	16
BEARD	2	BELIEVED	1
BEARS	197	BELIEVES	1

WORD	FREQ.	WORD	FREQ.
BELINDA	1	BILL	22
BELL	17	BILL'S	1
BELLE	2	BILLFOLD	1
BELLS	6	BILLS	5
BELLY	10	BILLY	69
BELLYACHE	1	BING	5
BELONGED	3	BINGO	37
BELOW	3	BINGOS	1
BELT	21	BIOGRAPHY	1
BELT'S	2	BIONIC	39
BELTS	5	BIONICS	8
BEN	9	BIRD	76
BEN'S	1	BIRD'S	1
BENCH	2	BIRDIES	2
BENCHES	2	BIRDS	27
BEND	7	BIRDSEED	1
BENDED*	4	BIRTH	1
BENDING	1	BIRTHDAY	98
BENEATH	1	BIRTHSTONE	1
BENGALS	2	BIT	66
BENJAMIN	2	BITE	28
BENT	3	BITED	1
BERET	9	BITES	5
BERETS	2	BITING	2
BERRIES	1	BITS	1
BERT	1	BITTY	4
BESIDE	11	BLACK	148
BESIDES	1	BLACKBIRDS	1
BESSIE	2	BLACKBOARD	1
BEST	71	BLACKHAWKS	2
BESTEST*	2	BLACKS	1
BET	19	BLACKTOP	4
BETH	1	BLADE	3
BETTED	1	BLAME	1
BETTER	88	BLANK	2
BETTY	11	BLANKET	4
BETWEEN	7	BLANKETS	2
BEVINGTON	1	BLANKS	1
BEWITCHED	3	BLAZE	1
BIB	3	BLEACHERS	1
BICYCLE	11	BLEEDING	3
BIDDLE	1	BLENDER	4
BIG	689	BLESS	1
BIGFOOT	24	BLEW	41
BIGFOOTS	1	BLIND	1
BIGGER	50	BLINDFOLD	2
BIGGEST	11	BLINDFOLDED	2
BIGS*	1	BLINKING	1
BIKE	101	BLOB	2
BIKES	13	BLOCK	19

WORD	FREQ.	WORD	FREQ.
BLOCKAGE	1	BONANZA	3
BLOCKED	1	BONE	24
BLOCKHEAD	1	BONEMAN	1
BLOCKING	2	BONES	14
BLOCKS	13	BONK	2
BLONDE	7	BONNET	1
BLOOD	32	BOO	11
BLOODY	3	BOOGER	8
BLOOMING	1	BOOK	117
BLOW	59	BOOKS.	45
BLOWED*	29	BOOM	33
BLOWING	6	BOOMED	1
BLOWN	1	BOONE	3
BLOWS	11	BOOP*	2
BLUE	127	BOOT	2
BLUEJEANS	1	BOOTH	1
BLUES	10	BOOTS	12
BLUFF	1	BORED	1
BLUISH	1	BORING	6
BLUSHING	1	BORN	16
BLUSTERY	1	BORROW	3
BLUTO	4	BORROWED	1
BO	4	BOSLEY	1
BOA	13	BOSS	13
BOARD	91	BOSTON	1
BOARDS	5	BOTH	105
BOARDWALK	2	BOTHER	1
BOAT	77	BOTHERING	2
BOATING	3	BOTHERS	2
BOATS	21	BOTTLE	21
BOB	16	BOTTLES	3
BOBBER	5	BOTTOM	45
BOBBIN	4	BOUGHT	51
BOBBY	19	BOUNCE	15
BOBBY'S	2	BOUNCED	7
BOBO	8	BOUNCES	9
BOBO'S	3	BOUNCING	6
BOBS	1	BOUNCY	2
BODY	15	BOUNDS	1
BODY'S	1	BOUT	1
BOIL	1	BOW	3
BOILING	3	BOWL	33
BOING	5	BOWL'S	1
BOLD	1	BOWLING	2
BOLOGNA	4	BOWLS	10
BOLT	1	BOWS	1
BOMB	34	BOX	55
BOMBER	1	BOXED	3
BOMBS	18	BOXES	8
BON	2	BOXING	10

WORD	FREQ.	WORD	FREQ.
BOY	348	BRIGHT	3
BOY'S	22	BRING	47
BOYFRIEND	10	BRINGED*	4
BOYFRIENDS	2	BRINGS	10
BOYS	60	BRITCHES	1
BOZO	32	BROKE	136
BOZO'S	4	BROKED*	5
BRACES	1	BROKEN	14
BRAD	5	BROKES*	1
BRADY	23	BRONCHITIS	1
BRAID	1	BRONTOSAURUS	1
BRAIDED	1	BROOK'S	1
BRAIDS	1	BROOKIE	1
BRAIN	7	BROOKS	1
BRAKE	5	BROOM	15
BRAKES	5	BROTHER	326
BRANCH	3	BROTHER'S	30
BRANCHES	6	BROTHERS	42
BRAND	2	BROUGHT	48
BRANDON	1	BROWN	88
BRANDY	1	BROWNIE	6
BRANG*	6	BROWNISH	1
BRANT	3	BROWNS	2
BRAUN	2	BROWS	1
BRAVE	2	BRUCE	1
BRAVER	2	BRUISE	5
BRAVEST	2	BRUISED	3
BREAD	16	BRUNG*	5
BREAK	46	BRUSH	7
BREAKED*	1	BRUSHED	1
BREAKER	4	BRUSHES	1
BREAKFAST	10	BRUSHING	1
BREAKING	8	BRUTUS	39
BREAKS	8	BRUTUS'	1
BREATH	1	BUBBLE	7
BREATHE	2	BUBBLES	5
BRENDA	2	BUBBLY	1
BRENT	2	BUBBS	3
BRETT	2	BUCK'S	1
BRETT'S	1	BUCKET	34
BRIAN	28	BUCKETS	13
BRIAN'S	2	BUCKLED	1
BRIANS	1	BUCKS	2
BRIAR	4	BUCKWHEAT	10
BRICK	23	BUDDING	1
BRICKED	1	BUDDY	4
BRICKS	36	BUFFALO	3
BRIDE	3	BUFFY	2
BRIDGE	47	BUG	3
BRIDGES	3	BUGGING	2

WORD	FREQ.	WORD	FREQ.
BUGGY	2	BUSCH	1
BUGS	82	BUSES	3
BUILD	49	BUSH	8
BUILDED*	8	BUSHES	11
BUILDING	48	BUSINESS	7
BUILDINGS	18	BUSSES	1
BUILDS	1	BUST	6
BUILT	34	BUSTED	16
BULB	8	BUSTING	1
BULBS	1	BUSTS	1
BULL	2	BUSY	3
BULL'S-EYE	1	BUT	1229
BULL'S-EYES	3	BUTCH	12
BULLDOG	4	BUTCHER	5
BULLET	4	BUTS	1
BULLETS	4	BUTT	9
BULLS	5	BUTTER	20
BUM	1	BUTTERFLIES	2
BUMBLE	2	BUTTERFLY	13
BUMP	10	BUTTON	35
BUMPED	8	BUTTONED	3
BUMPER	3	BUTTONS	27
BUMPING	1	BUY	66
BUMPS	5	BUYED*	1
BUMPY	5	BUYER	5
BUMS	1	BUYING	2
BUNCH	83	BUYS	10
BUNCHES	1	BUZZ	6
BUNK	11	BY	248
BUNKER	2	BYE	8
BUNNIES	3	C	10
BUNNY	93	CABANA	1
BUNNY'S	1	CABBAGE	5
BUNS	4	CABIN	10
BUNT	2	CABINET	5
BURGER	4	CABINETS	1
BURGLARS	2	CABLE	2
BURIED	12	CACKLEBURG	2
BURN	13	CACTUS	1
BURNED	19	CADILLAC	1
BURNEDED	1	CAFETERIA	1
BURNETT	3	CAGE	31
BURNING	7	CAGES	5
BURNS	1	CAIN	1
BURNT	2	CAKE	30
BURRO	1	CAKES	6
BURST	1	CALF	1
BURT	2	CALIFORNIA	5
BURY	8	CALL	82
BUS	66	CALLED	151

WORD	FREQ.	WORD	FREQ.
CALLING	25	CARES	4
CALLS	18	CAREY	2
CAME	579	CARIBBEAN	1
CAMED	3	CARL	2
CAMELS	2	CARLSBAD	1
CAMERA	3	CARNIVAL	1
CAMERAS	1	CARNIVALS	1
CAMP	13	CAROL	8
CAMPER	25	CAROLYN	2
CAMPGROUND	1	CARP	1
CAMPING	26	CARPENTER	1
CAMPS	3	CARPETING	4
CAN	889	CARRIAGE	2
CAN'T	601	CARRIE	1
CANADA	2	CARRIER	1
CANARY	1	CARRIES	4
CANDIES	3	CARROT	8
CANDLE	2	CARROTS	10
CANDLES	2	CARRY	12
CANDY	140	CARRYING	5
CANDYLAND	10	CARS	66
CANE	1	CART	2
CANES	10	CARTER	1
CANNED	1	CARTOON	51
CANNON	4	CARTOONS	124
CANNOT	1	CARTWHEEL	4
CANOE	3	CARTWHEELS	6
CANS	9	CARVED	1
CANTEEN	1	CASCADE	2
CANYON	4	CASE	15
CAP	6	CASES	2
CAPE	6	CASH	1
CAPER	1	CASPER	28
CAPITAL	3	CASPER'S	2
CAPITALS	1	CASS	2
CAPS	2	CAST	11
CAPSULE	2	CASTED*	3
CAPTAIN	11	CASTLE	20
CAPTAINS	3	CASTLES	3
CAPTURE	6	CASTOR	1
CAPTURED	9	CAT	131
CAR	173	CAT'S	5
CARBURETOR	1	CAT'S-EYE	4
CARD	150	CATCH	174
CARDBOARD	3	CATCHED*	7
CARDINALS	1	CATCHER	12
CARDS	152	CATCHER'S	1
CARE	24	CATCHERS	4
CAREERS	1	CATCHES	22
CAREFUL	6	CATCHING	14

WORD	FREQ.	WORD	FREQ.
CATERPILLAR	1	CHANNEL	21
CATFISH	4	CHANNELS	1
CATHERINE	1	CHAPMAN	1
CATHY	4	CHAPS	2
CATS	31	CHAR	1
CATSUP	3	CHARACTER	5
CAUGHT	125	CHARACTERS	3
CAUSE	109	CHARADES	1
CAUSING	1	CHARGE	2
CAVE	19	CHARGED	1
CAVED	1	CHARGING	1
CAVEMEN	1	CHARLENE	1
CAVERNS	1	CHARLES	3
CAVES	6	CHARLIE	58
CAVITIES	2	CHARLIE'S	8
CB	2	CHARLIES	6
CB'S	2	CHARLOTTE	3
CBS	1	CHART	1
CC	1	CHASE	32
CEDAR	1	CHASED	18
CEILING	7	CHASERS	1
CELEBRATE	3	CHASES	9
CELEBRATED	2	CHASING	25
CELERY	1	CHATTERING	1
CELLAR	5	CHEAT	3
CEMENT	8	CHEATED	1
CEMENTY*	1	CHEATING	1
CEMETERY	3	CHECK	9
CENTER	6	CHECKED	11
CENTS	4	CHECKER	5
CEREAL	13	CHECKERS	35
CERTAIN	3	CHECKMATE	1
CHA	2	CHECKS	4
CHAD	2	CHEEP	2
CHAIN	10	CHEEPIES	1
CHAINED	2	CHEERIO	4
CHAINS	2	CHEERIOS	2
CHAIR	256	CHEESE	23
CHAIRS	36	CHEF	5
CHALK	5	CHER	5
CHALKBOARD	5	CHERRIES	8
CHALMER	2	CHERRY	5
CHAMP	1	CHERYL	1
CHAMPAIGN	1	CHESS	5
CHAMPION	2	CHEST	7
CHAMPIONS	2	CHESTS	1
CHANCE	10	CHEVY	1
CHANGE	10	CHEW	2
CHANGED	9	CHEWBACCA	1
CHANGES	1	CHEWED	2

WORD	FREQ.	WORD	FREQ.
CHEWING	3	CHUCK	13
CHICAGO	11	CHUCKIE'S	1
CHICK	3	CHUCKY	9
CHICKEN	48	CHUGGY	1
CHICKEN'S	1	CHUM	1
CHICKENS	15	CHUNKS	1
CHICKS	5	CHURCH	23
CHIEF	7	CHUTE	3
CHILD	4	CHUTES	6
CHILD'S	1	CIDER	8
CHILDREN	18	CIGAR	3
CHILDREN'S	5	CIGARETTE	2
CHILLER	1	CIGARS	1
CHIMFANZINE	2	CINCH	1
CHIMNEY	27	CINCINNATI	4
CHIMNEYS	2	CINCO	1
CHIMPANZEE	1	CINDERELLA	22
CHIN	37	CINDY	14
CHINA	6	CINDY'S	2
CHINA'S	1	CIRCLE	54
CHINESE	2	CIRCLES	16
CHINNY	12	CIRCUS	17
CHIP	3	CIRCUSES	1
CHIPMUNK	1	CITIES	1
CHIPMUNKS	7	CITY	25
CHIPPED	1	CLAP	3
CHIPPER	2	CLARA	1
CHIPS	4	CLARK	3
CHOCOLATE	14	CLASS	34
CHOICE	1	CLASS'	1
CHOICES	1	CLASSROOM	4
CHOKING	2	CLAUS'S	22
CHOMP	1	CLAWS	1
CHOO	6	CLAY	12
CHOO-CHOO	1	CLEAN	28
CHOOSE	7	CLEANED	7
CHOP	2	CLEANER	1
CHOPPED	14	CLEANING	6
CHOPPER	3	CLEANS	1
CHORES	2	CLEAR	25
CHOSE	4	CLEATS	1
CHOSEN	2	CLICK	17
CHRIS	30	CLIFF	6
CHRIS'S	3	CLIFFS	1
CHRISSY	6	CLIMB	25
CHRISTA	1	CLIMBED	19
CHRISTMAS	100	CLIMBING	11
CHRISTOPHER	11	CLIMBS	10
CHRISTY	19	CLIP	2
CHRYSLER	3	CLIPS	1

WORD	FREQ.	WORD	FREQ.
CLOCK	21	COLLEGE	11
CLOCKS	1	COLLIE	5
CLOGS	1	COLONIAL	1
CLOSE	49	COLOR	91
CLOSED	16	COLORADO	6
CLOSER	12	COLORED	21
CLOSES	1	COLORING	11
CLOSEST	8	COLORS	48
CLOSET	28	COLTRAIN	1
CLOSING	5	COLTS	1
CLOTHER'S	1	COLUMBIAN	1
CLOTHES	53	COLUMBUS	1
CLOUD	3	COLUMINY	3
CLOUDS	6	COLUMY	1
CLOUDY	1	COMANCHE	1
CLOWN	17	COMB	4
CLOWNS	12	COME	389
CLUB	16	COMED*	17
CLUBHOUSE	2	COMES	195
CLUBS	2	COMETS	1
CLUCK	1	COMFORTABLE	2
CLUNKED	1	COMIC	1
COACH	6	COMICS	4
COACH'S	2	COMING	108
COACHES	1	COMMAND	1
COAL.	2	COMMANDER	3
COASTER	28	COMMANDERS	1
COASTERS	7	COMMERCIAL	13
COAT	38	COMMISSION	7
COATS	9	COMMUNION	1
COBRA	3	COMMUNITY	2
COCA-COLA	1	COMPACTOR	2
COCKER	1	COMPANY	7
COCOA	3	COMPARED	1
COFFEE	8	COMPETING	2
COFFIN	1	COMPETITION	1
COIN	2	CONCESSION	1
COKE	6	CONCRETE	3
COLD	86	CONDUCTOR	1
COLDER	3	CONE	48
COLE	1	CONES	6
COLGATE	1	CONFERENCE	1
COLLAPSED	1	CONK	1
COLLAPSES	1	CONNIE	2
COLLAR	3	CONSTRICTOR	13
COLLARS	1	CONSTRUCTION	4
COLLECT	3	CONTACT	1
COLLECTION	3	CONTAINER	1
COLLEEN	1	CONTEMPORARY	1
COLLEEN'S	1	CONTEST	2

WORD	FREQ.	WORD	FREQ.
CONTESTS	1	COUNT	50
CONTINUE	1	COUNTED	5
CONTINUED	2	COUNTER	1
CONTRAPTION	1	COUNTING	10
CONTROL	5	COUNTRY	12
CONTROLLING	1	COUNTS	12
CONTROLS	2	COUNTY	6
CONVERSATION	1	COUPLE	33
COO	2	COURSE	6
COOK	16	COURT	7
COOKED	8	COURTS	2
COOKER	1	COUSIN	59
COOKIE	24	COUSIN'S	11
COOKIE'S	2	COUSINS	31
COOKIES	19	COVER	6
COOKING	12	COVERED	9
COOKOUTS	1	COVERS	10
COOKS	3	COW	26
COOL	14	COW'S	3
COOLS	1	COWARD	1
COONS	1	COWBOY	22
COOPER	2	COWBOYS	16
COOTIE	3	COWS	16
COP	6	COYOTE	8
COPS	4	CRAB	13
COPY	3	CRABBY	1
CORD	1	CRABS	3
COREY	1	CRACK	3
CORKY	3	CRACKED	6
CORKY'S	1	CRACKER	2
CORN	10	CRACKERS	4
CORNER	23	CRACKING	3
CORNY	1	CRACKS	1
CORPMAN	1	CRAIG	2
CORRAL	4	CRANE	1
CORRECTING	1	CRANK	1
CORRIE	1	CRAPPIE	1
CORVETTE	2	CRAPPY	1
COST	3	CRASH	14
COSTS	2	CRASHED	18
COSTUME	3	CRASHES	1
COSTUMES	6	CRASHING	1
COTTAGE	10	CRAWDAD	2
COTTON	8	CRAWDADS	1
COUCH	18	CRAWL	2
COUCHES	2	CRAWLED	4
COUGAR	3	CRAWLER	2
COUGH	1	CRAWLERS	2
COULD	291	CRAWLING	3
COULDN'T	176	CRAWLS	2

WORD	FREQ.	WORD	FREQ.
CRAYFISH	1	CRYSTAL	3
CRAYON	4	CRYSTALS	1
CRAYONS	13	CUB	1
CRAZIEST	1	CUCKOO	2
CRAZY	21	CUDDLES	1
CREAM	206	CUDDLY	2
CREAM'S	1	CUFFS	1
CREATES	1	CUMBERLAND	3
CREATURE	2	CUNNINGHAM	3
CREATURES	4	CUP	12
CREEK	3	CUPCAKES	2
CREEP	1	CUPS	7
CREEPED*	1	CURDS	4
CREEPING	2	CURE	1
CREEPS	4	CURIOUS	1
CREEPY	4	CURLING	1
CREPT	1	CURLS	4
CRIB	3	CURLY	4
CRICKET	4	CURSE	8
CRICKETS	2	CURSED	1
CRIED	10	CURSES	1
CRIES	8	CURTAIN	5
CRIME	6	CURTAINS	14
CRIMINALS	1	CURVE	2
CRISPY	2	CURVED	2
CRITTERS	1	CURVES	2
CROAK	1	CURVING	1
CROCODILE	2	CURVY*	1
CROOK	2	CUSHIONS	2
CROOKED	3	CUSS	1
CROOKS	6	CUSSES	1
CROSS	19	CUT	63
CROSSED	1	CUTE	13
CROSSES	1	CUTS	2
CROSSING	4	CUTTED*	2
CROSSINGS	1	CUTTING	6
CROWD	2	CYCLE	4
CROWDED	1	CYCLES	3
CROWN	4	CYLON	4
CRUEL	1	CYLONS	7
CRUISER	1	D	6
CRUMBLE	1	DAB	4
CRUNCH	1	DABA	1
CRUNCHED	1	DAD	426
CRUNCHING	4	DAD'S	39
CRUSHED	2	DADA	4
CRUSHES	1	DADDIES	2
CRUTCHES	4	DADDY	107
CRY	11	DADDY-O	4
CRYING	24	DADDY'S	25

WORD	FREQ.	WORD	FREQ.
DADS	7	DAVIS	2
DAFFY	19	DAWN	4
DAG NABBIT	1	DAY	231
DAILY	1	DAYS	83
DAIRY	13	DAYTIME	4
DAISIES	2	DEACT*	1
DAISY	6	DEAD	38
DAISY'S	1	DEAF	2
DAKOTA	2	DEAL	2
DALLAS	6	DEALER	1
DAM	4	DEAN	2
DAN	10	DEANA	5
DAN'S	3	DEANN	2
DANCE	5	DEAR	17
DANCED	5	DEARS	1
DANCER'S	1	DEATH	1
DANCES	3	DEBBIE	5
DANCING	5	DEBBIE'S	6
DANDELIONS	20	DECIDE	2
DANG	2	DECIDED	13
DANGER	4	DECISION	1
DANGEROUS	4	DECK	7
DANIEL	3	DECKS	2
DANIELLE	1	DECORATED	1
DANNY	5	DECORATION	2
DAPHNE	1	DEE	4
DAR	1	DEED	1
DARBY	1	DEEP	15
DARE	1	DEEPER	3
DARK	22	DEER	10
DARKEST	1	DEERS*	1
DARLA	1	DEFENSE	1
DARLENE	1	DEFFENBAUGH	1
DARLING	1	DEGREES	1
DARN	6	DELANEY	1
DARNELL	3	DELCO	2
DARREN	8	DELIRIOUS	1
DARREN'S	4	DEMON	3
DART	8	DENISE	2
DARTH	2	DENNIS	7
DARTS	11	DENTED	1
DARYL	1	DENTIST	4
DATE	1	DEPENDS	1
DAUGHTER	3	DEPUTY	1
DAUGHTERS	2	DERBY	4
DAVE	2	DERRICK	1
DAVE'S	1	DESERT	2
DAVID	10	DESIGNS	1
DAVID'S	1	DESK	16
DAVIDSON	1	DESKSTAR	1

WORD	FREQ.	WORD	FREQ.
DESSERT	1	DISH	3
DESTROYER	1	DISHES	38
DESTROYS	1	DISHWASHER	1
DETECTIVE	2	DISNEY	18
DETECTIVES	3	DISNEY'S	1
DEVIL	6	DISNEYLAND	5
DEVILS	1	DISNEYWORLD	4
DEVLIN	1	DITCH	2
DEWEY	4	DITTY	1
DIAGONAL	2	DIVE	6
DIAL	6	DIVER	1
DIAMOND	3	DIVERS	1
DIANE	5	DIVING	7
DIANE'S	2	DIVISION	1
DIAPER	4	DIVORCED	2
DIAPERS	4	DIXIE	8
DIARY	1	DIXON	2
DICE	60	DIZZY	2
DICES*	5	DO	714
DICK	7	DOC	3
DID	339	DOCK	4
DIDN'T	528	DOCTOR	50
DIE	15	DOCTOR'S	2
DIED	40	DOCTORS	1
DIES	3	DODGE	2
DIET	2	DODGEBALL	1
DIFFERENCE	2	DODGER	2
DIFFERENT	107	DOE	2
DIG	11	DOES	124
DIGGED*	3	DOESN'T	94
DIGGING	3	DOG	389
DILLY	1	DOG'S	33
DIME	3	DOGGIE	20
DING	7	DOGGIE'S	1
DINGS	1	DOGHOUSE	6
DINKY	1	DOGS	73
DINNER	20	DOING	106
DINO	6	DOLL	34
DINOSAUR	23	DOLLAR	33'
DINOSAUR'S	2	DOLLARS	47
DINOSAURS	12	DOLLIES	2
DIP	2	DOLLS	21
DIPPER	2	DOLLY	5
DIRECTION	2	DOLPHIN	3
DIRECTIONS	2	DOLPHINS	3
DIRT	25	DOME'S	1
DIRTY	17	DOMES	1
DISAPPEARED	6	DOMINOES	5
DISGUISE	2	DON	6
DISGUISED	1	DON'T	1697

WORD	FREQ.	WORD	FREQ.
DONALD	24	DRAPERIES	1
DONE	114	DRAPES	1
DONED*	2	DRAW	55
DONG	4	DRAWED*	7
DONKEY	12	DRAWER	7
DONKEYS	4	DRAWERS	1
DONNA'S	1	DRAWING	9
DONNOR	2	DRAWS	1
DONNY	19	DREAM	7
DONUT	3	DREAMED	3
DONUTS	5	DREAMING	5
DOO	15	DREAMS	1
DOO'S	1	DRESS	32
DOOBY	1	DRESSED	29
DOODY	12	DRESSER	3
DOOR	203	DRESSERS	4
DOORBELL	2	DRESSES	6
DOORS	14	DRESSING	4
DOORWAY'S	1	DREW	2
DOPE	4	DREWED*	1
DOREENA	1	DRIBBLE	1
DOROTHY	26	DRIED	4
DOROTHY'S	2	DRIES	1
DOS	1	DRILL	1
DOT	10	DRINK	19
DOT'S	1	DRINKING	6
DOTS	5	DRINKS	6
DOUBLE	16	DRIP	3
DOUBLES	1	DRIPPING	6
DOUBLING	1	DRIPS	1
DOUG	6	DRIVE	16
DOUGH	10	DRIVED*	2
DOUGIE	2	DRIVER	5
DOVE	1	DRIVES	10
DOWN	1234	DRIVEWAY	4
DOWNED	1	DRIVING	15
DOWNS	3	DROP	21
DOWNSTAIRS	23	DROPPED	20
DOZEN	1	DROPPING	3
DOZENS	1	DROPS	11
DRACULA	9	DROVE	11
DRACULA'S	1	DROWN	3
DRAG	4	DROWNED	18
DRAGGED	1	DROWNING	3
DRAGGING	1	DROWNS	2
DRAGON	10	DRUM	2
DRAGONS	1	DRUMMER	1
DRAIN	2	DRUMS	3
DRAINED	4	DRUNK	7
DRANK	5	DRY	8

WORD	FREQ.	WORD	FREQ.
DRYWALL	1	EAST	1
DUB	1	EASTER	12
DUCK	139	EASY	28
DUCK'S	1	EAT	220
DUCKER*	1	EATEN	6
DUCKIES	1	EATER	2
DUCKING	1	EATING	212
DUCKS	23	EATS	29
DUDE	2	EBBIE	1
DUEL	1	EDDIE	1
DUG	3	EDDIE'S	3
DUGOUT	1	EDGE	3
DUKE	4	EDITH	3
DUKES	8	EELS	1
DULUTH	1	EGG	23
DUMB	22	EGGHEAD	2
DUMBEST	1	EGGROLLS	1
DUMBO	3	EGGS	23
DUMMIES	2	EIFFEL	3
DUMP	4	EIGHT	66
DUMPED	1	EIGHTEEN	13
DUMPING	1	EIGHTH	2
DUMPTY	16	EIGHTS	2
DUNGEON	3	EILEEN	3
DUNK	1	EITHER	52
DUNKED	2	ELASTIC	2
DUO	3	ELBOW	2
DURING	4	ELECTRIC	8
DUST	2	ELECTRICITY	4
DWARFS*	1	ELEPHANT	10
DWAYNE	3	ELEPHANTS	12
DYKE	3	ELEVATOR	10
DYNAMIC	3	ELEVATORS	1
DYNAMITE	8	ELEVEN	21
DYNAMUTT	2	ELEVENTH	1
E	4	ELLA	1
EACH	110	ELLEN	1
EAGLE	5	ELLER	3
EAGLES	1	ELMER	2
EAR	6	ELSE	283
EARL	2	ELSE'S	8
EARLY	15	ELVIS	19
EARN	3	ELWOOD	2
EARPHONES	1	ELZROTH	1
EARRING	1	ELZROTH'S	1
EARRINGS	1	EM	24
EARS	14	EMBARRASSED	1
EARTH	2	EMERGENCY	27
EARTHQUAKE	2	EMMA	1
EASIER	1	EMPIRE	1

WORD	FREQ.	WORD	FREQ.
EMPTY	2	EXERCISES	1
END	144	EXIST	1
ENDED	3	EXIT	3
ENDING	4	EXPEDITION	1
ENDS	2	EXPENSIVE	1
ENEMIES	1	EXPERIMENT	2
ENEMY	3	EXPLAIN	5
ENGINE	9	EXPLODE	5
ENGINES	1	EXPLODED	7
ENJOY	2	EXPLODES	1
ENOUGH	30	EXPLORE	1
ENVELOPE	1	EXTINGUISH	1
EQUAL	10	EXTRA	2
EQUALS	1	EXTRAS	1
ERASE	6	EYE	48
ERASER	6	EYEBALLS	1
ERASERS	1	EYEBROWS	1
ERIC	8	EYEGLASS	1
ERIC'S	2	EYEGLASSES	1
ERICKSON	2	EYELIDS	1
ERN	2	EYES	92
ERNIE	4	F	6
ERUPTED	1	FACE	74
ESCAPE	6	FACED	1
ESP	1	FACES	8
ESPECIALLY	11	FACING	2
ESTHER'S	2	FACT	1
EVE	8	FACTORY	4
EVEL	13	FAINTED	2
EVEN	125	FAINTS	1
EVENING	2	FAIR	18
EVER	82	FAIRGROUND	1
EVERY	193	FAIRS	1
EVERYBODY	111	FAIRY	9
EVERYBODY'S	9	FAKE	8
EVERYDAY	3	FAKES	1
EVERYONE	21	FAKING	1
EVERYONE'S	1	FALL	73
EVERYTHING	106	FALLED*	9
EVERYWHERE	8	FALLEN	1
EVIDENTLY	1	FALLING	19
EVIL	1	FALLS	35
EXACTLY	3	FAMILY	33
EXCEPT	96	FAMILY'S	1
EXCITE	1	FAMOUS	1
EXCITED	2	FAN	3
EXCITING	11	FANCY	1
EXCITINGEST*	1	FANNING	1
EXCUSE	6	FANTASY	1
EXERCISE	1	FAR	56

WORD	FREQ.	WORD	FREQ.
FARAH	1	FIELD	32
FARM	25	FIELDERS	3
FARMER	14	FIFTEEN	27
FARMERS	2	FIFTEENTH	1
FARMS	1	FIFTH	17
FARTHER	11	FIFTIES	1
FARTHEST	1	FIFTY	24
FARTS	1	FIGHT	66
FASHIONED	1	FIGHTED*	5
FAST	126	FIGHTERS	3
FASTBALL	1	FIGHTING	42
FASTEN	1	FIGHTS	26
FASTER	31	FIGURE	4
FASTEST	4	FIGURED	1
FAT	41	FIGURES	1
FATHER	85	FILES	1
FATHER'S	15	FILL	3
FATSO	1	FILLED	10
FATTER	1	FILLS	1
FATTY	1	FILM	10
FAUCET	1	FILMS	3
FAULT	2	FIN	1
FAVORITE	138	FINALLY	36
FAWCETT	1	FIND	126
FEATHERS	2	FINDED*	1
FEATHERY	1	FINDING	4
FEBRUARY	3	FINDS	15
FED	8	FINE	3
FEED	27	FINGER	27
FEEDED*	3	FINGERNAIL	2
FEEDING	3	FINGERS	12
FEEL	14	FINISH	7
FEELED*	2	FINISHED	12
FEELING	2	FINISHES	1
FEELINGS	1	FIRE	127
FEELS	8	FIREBALL	1
FEET	77	FIRECRACKER	7
FEETS*	1	FIREHOUSE	5
FELIX	1	FIREMAN	5
FELL	194	FIREMAN'S	1
FELLOW	1	FIREPLACE	4
FELT	10	FIREPLACES	1
FENCE	21	FIRES	1
FENCES	2	FIRETRUCK	2
FERRIS	14	FIRETRUCKS	1
FESTIVAL	5	FIREWORKS	1
FETCH	1	FIRING	2
FEW	22	FIRST	350
FIB	1	FIRSTLY	1
FICTION	1	FISH	135

WORD	FREQ.	WORD	FREQ.
FISHED	3	FLOUR	2
FISHERMAN	3	FLOWER	40
FISHES	8	FLOWERS	178
FISHING	60	FLOWN	1
FISHY	3	FLOYD	1
FIST	1	FLU	1
FIT	8	FLUFFY	3
FITS	3	FLUNK	2
FITTED	1	FLUSH	1
FIVE	199	FLUSHED	1
FIVES	1	FLUTE	1
FIX	20	FLY	50
FIXED	30	FLYING	20
FIXES	2	FLYNN	1
FIXING	12	FOLD	2
FLAG	20	FOLDED	5
FLAGS	12	FOLKS	3
FLAMES	1	FOLLOW	16
FLAP	1	FOLLOWED	11
FLASH	4	FOLLOWING	8
FLASHLIGHT	1	FOLLOWS	7
FLAT	17	FONZ	10
FLATTEN	3	FONZIE	6
FLAVOR	1	FONZIE'S	1
FLEAS	1	FOOD	74
FLEW	26	FOOL	5
FLIED	3	FOOT	59
FLIES	17	FOOTBALL	93
FLING	1	FOOTBALL'S	1
FLINGED	1	FOOTBALLS	1
FLINTSTONE	28	FOOTSTEPS	3
FLINTSTONES	1	FOR	627
FLIP	12	FORCE	3
FLIPPED	6	FORCED	1
FLIPPER	7	FOREST	20
FLIPPING	2	FOREVER	2
FLIPS	5	FORGET	154
FLO	1	FORGETTING	2
FLOAT	13	FORGOT	134
FLOATED	3	FORK	3
FLOATING	6	FORKS	1
FLOODED	2	FORM	1
FLOOR	45	FORMULA	3
FLOORS	2	FORT	2
FLOPPED	1	FORTH	15
FLOPPING	2	FORTUNATELY	9
FLOPPY	1	FORTY	18
FLOPS	1	FORWARD	3
FLORA	1	FORWARDS	1
FLORIDA	25	FOSSIL	2

WORD	FREQ.	WORD	FREQ.
FOSSILS	1	FROG	22
FOUGHT	6	FROGGIES	1
FOUL	8	FROGS	4
FOUND	115	FROM	236
FOUNDED*	1	FRONT	50
FOUNTAIN	1	FRONTWARDS	2
FOUNTAINS	1	FROSTIES	1
FOUR	254	FROSTING	3
FOUR-NINETY-FIVE	1	FROSTY	10
FOURTEEN	14	FROZE	4
FOURTH	9	FROZEN	34
FOWLER	2	FRUIT	6
FOX	61	FRUITS	3
FOXES	8	FRY	1
FOXY	1	FRYING	3
FOZZI	3	FUDD	3
FRACTURED	2	FUDGE	3
FRAME	3	FULL	20
FRANCIS	1	FUN	168
FRANCISCO	1	FUNERAL	1
FRANK	1	FUNNER*	1
FRANKENSTEIN	5	FUNNEST*	7
FRANKFURTER	1	FUNNIES	3
FRANKIE	5	FUNNIEST	10
FRASER	3	FUNNY	160
FREAK	2	FUR	4
FRECKLES	5	FURNITURE	4
FRED	17	FURRY	1
FRED'S	2	FURTHER	2
FREDDIE	1	FUSES	1
FREDDY	3	FUTURE	1
FREE	18	FUZZ	1
FREEZE	10	FUZZY	2
FREEZED*	1	G	7
FREEZEMAN	1	GAIL	3
FREEZER	1	GALACTICA	7
FREEZING	6	GALEN	5
FREIGHTERS	1	GALLERY	2
FRENCH	3	GAME	359
FRIDAY	23	GAME'S	1
FRIED	3	GAMES	114
FRIEND	128	GANG	10
FRIEND'S	28	GAR	4
FRIENDLY	13	GAR'S	1
FRIENDS	108	GARAGE	21
FRIES	1	GARAGES	1
FRIGHTENED	7	GARBAGE	5
FRISBEE	4	GARDEN	7
FRITZ	8	GARDENER	1
FRITZIE	2	GARDENERS	1

WORD	FREQ.	WORD	FREQ.
GARDENS	1	GIVEN	1
GARFIELD	2	GIVES	24
GARGOYLE	2	GIVING	10
GARRETT	4	GIZMO	1
GARTER	2	GIZZARD	2
GARY	2	GLAD	21
GAS	24	GLASS	16
GASOLINE	1	GLASSES	11
GASTON	1	GLENN	3
GATE	7	GLITTER	1
GATES	2	GLORIA	1
GATHERED	2	GLOVE	6
GAUGE	1	GLOVES	4
GAVE	116	GLOW	1
GAZELLE	1	GLOWS	1
GEAR	1	GLUE	6
GEE	2	GLUES	1
GENERAL	3	GNAW	1
GENIE	1	GNIP-GNOP	2
GENTLEMEN	3	GO	1884
GENTLY	2	GOAL	27
GEORGE	7	GOALS	3
GEORGIE	3	GOAT	55
GERMAN	4	GOATS	23
GERMANY	1	GOB	10
GET	2067	GOBBLE	2
GETS	349	GOBBLED	2
GETTING	109	GOBS	1
GHOST	83	GOD	7
GHOSTS	22	GODFATHER	1
GIANT	60	GODMOTHER	3
GIANTS	5	GODZILLA	41
GIDDY	2	GODZILLAS	2
GIFT	3	GOED*	2
GIGGLES	1	GOES	479
GIGGLING	1	GOING	915
GILLIGAN	11	GOINGED*	1
GILLIGAN'S	9	GOLD	23
GINA'S	1	GOLDAR	4
GINGER	7	GOLDEN	3
GINGERBREAD	37	GOLDFISH	3
GIRAFFE	3	GOLDILOCKS	87
GIRAFFES	4	GOLDMAN	2
GIRL	351	GOLF	8
GIRL'S	24	GONE	52
GIRLFRIEND	25	GONG	3
GIRLIE	1	GOO	3
GIRLS	91	GOOBER	1
GIVE	117	GOOCHIE	2
GIVED*	1	GOOD	202

WORD	FREQ.	WORD	FREQ.
GOOD−BYE	12	GRAPES	1
GOODER*	1	GRAS	4
GOODEST*	2	GRASS	44
GOODIE	3	GRAVE	8
GOODIES	4	GRAVEL	2
GOODS	2	GRAVEYARD	11
GOOF	1	GRAY	8
GOOFED	1	GRAYISH	1
GOOFING	1	GRAYS	2
GOOFS	1	GREASE	1
GOOFY	4	GREAT	55
GOONS	1	GREATER	1
GOOSE	45	GREATEST	3
GORDON	7	GREEN	98
GORDON'S	2	GREENISH	1
GORDY	1	GREENS	1
GORGO	5	GREG	18
GORILLA	20	GREGS	1
GORILLAS	5	GRENADES	2
GOSH	16	GREW	10
GOT	2689	GRIFFIN	1
GOTS*	105	GRIFFITH	3
GOVERNMENT	1	GRINCH	4
GRAB	5	GRIND	1
GRABBED	9	GRINDED*	2
GRABBING	3	GRINDING	3
GRABS	2	GRINNING	2
GRAD	1	GRIZZLY	4
GRADE	35	GROCERIES	6
GRADERS	9	GROCERY	4
GRADES	1	GROSS	2
GRAM	1	GROUCH	3
GRAMMA	40	GROUND	63
GRAMMA'S	15	GROUNDED	1
GRAMMAS	1	GROUP	8
GRAMPA	8	GROVER	3
GRAMPA'S	1	GROVER'S	2
GRAND	13	GROW	17
GRANDFATHER	4	GROWED*	3
GRANDMA	118	GROWING	6
GRANDMA'S	70	GROWL	1
GRANDMAS	1	GROWLING	2
GRANDMOTHER	27	GROWN	5
GRANDPA	38	GROWS	3
GRANDPA'S	7	GRUFF	13
GRANDPARENTS	1	GUARD	2
GRANDPAS	2	GUARDING	2
GRANGE	1	GUARDS	1
GRANNY	2	GUESS	49
GRAPE	1	GUESSED	2

WORD	FREQ.	WORD	FREQ.
GUESSES	2	HAND'S	1
GUESSING	1	HANDCUFFS	1
GUEST	5	HANDED	3
GUESTS	3	HANDKERCHIEF	3
GUIDE	2	HANDLE	9
GUIDES	1	HANDLEBARS	3
GUITAR	4	HANDLES	1
GULF	1	HANDOFF	2
GUM	12	HANDS	84
GUMBALL	1	HANESWORTH	1
GUMDROPS	2	HANG	15
GUN	44	HANGED	9
GUNFIGHTS	1	HANGERS	1
GUNNY	1	HANGING	21
GUNS	31	HANGS	1
GUNSMOKE	1	HAPPEN	10
GUS	11	HAPPENED	69
GUSTO	1	HAPPENING	1
GUTS	1	HAPPENS	9
GUY	221	HAPPILY	2
GUY'S	11	HAPPINESS	1
GUYS	160	HAPPY	37
GYM	32	HARD	182
GYMNASTICS	5	HARDER	2
GYMS	1	HARDEST	5
GYPSY	2	HARDLY	25
H	4	HARMONY	1
HAD	1081	HARPOONS	2
HADN'T	2	HART	4
HAINES	2	HAS	531
HAIR	112	HASN'T	3
HAIR'S	1	HASWELL	1
HAIRS	1	HAT	38
HAIRY	5	HATCHED	2
HALF	61	HATCHET	2
HALFWAY	1	HATCHING	1
HALL	4	HATE	20
HALLOWEEN	19	HATED	4
HALLWAY	3	HATES	11
HALO	1	HATING	1
HALTER	1	HATS	8
HALVES	2	HATTER	1
HAM	3	HAUNTED	29
HAMBURGER	3	HAUS	2
HAMBURGERS	2	HAVE	1691
HAMMER	10	HAVEN'T	48
HAMMERS	4	HAVING	44
HAMSTER	2	HAWAII	4
HAMSTERS	4	HAWAIIAN	1
HAND	142	HAWK	3

WORD	FREQ.	WORD	FREQ.
HAY	13	HELPER	1
HAYRIDE	2	HELPERS	1
HAYRIDES	1	HELPING	16
HAYSTACK	2	HELPS	14
HAYWORTH	12	HEM	1
HAZZARD	8	HEN	4
HAZZARDS	1	HENS	2
HE	4795	HEP	1
HE'D	13	HER	875
HE'LL	45	HERD	1
HE'S	555	HERE	482
HEAD	165	HERE'S	84
HEADACHE	8	HERO	2
HEADED	1	HEROES	3
HEADER	1	HERS	15
HEADING	1	HERSELF	13
HEADLESS	3	HEY	160
HEADLIGHTS	1	HI	129
HEADS	23	HIBERNATE	2
HEALED	1	HICCUP	2
HEALTHIER	1	HICCUPS	1
HEALTHY	1	HID	22
HEAR	82	HIDDEN	1
HEARD	85	HIDE	112
HEARED*	1	HIDE-A-BED	1
HEARING	1	HIDEOUT	2
HEARS	8	HIDES	26
HEART	19	HIDING	8
HEART'S	2	HIGH	73
HEARTS	16	HIGHCHAIR	2
HEATHER	7	HIGHER	16
HEATHER'S	2	HIGHEST	9
HEATHERS	1	HIGHLAND	4
HEATING	2	HIGHWAY	2
HEAVEN	3	HIKE	16
HEAVIER	1	HIKED	1
HEAVY	23	HIKES	3
HEBREW	1	HIKING	4
HECK	7	HILDA	2
HEELS	2	HILL	46
HEIGHTS	2	HILLS	10
HELD	2	HILLSIDE	2
HELICOPTER	13	HILLY	2
HELIUM	1	HIM	1058
HELL	1	HIM'S*	3
HELLO	49	HIMSELF	9
HELMET	4	HIND	1
HELMETS	5	HINKLE	7
HELP	82	HINKLE'S	1
HELPED	40	HINKLES	1

WORD	FREQ.	WORD	FREQ.
HIPPOPOTAMUS	4	HOOKS	1
HIPPOS	1	HOOP	7
HIRE	1	HOOPER	1
HIRES	1	HOOPING	1
HIS	1060	HOORAY	1
HISSELF*	13	HOOSKERDOO	1
HIT	284	HOOTCHIE	2
HITS	46	HOP	13
HITTED*	1	HOPE	12
HITTING	12	HOPING	1
HIVE	2	HOPPED	7
HO	8	HOPPING	4
HOBBY	4	HOPS	3
HOCKEY	18	HOPSCOTCH	5
HOG	6	HORN	3
HOGAN	2	HORNER	2
HOGAN'S	3	HORNS	12
HOKEY-POKEY	1	HORSE	46
HOLD	52	HORSEBACK	4
HOLDED*	5	HORSEMAN	3
HOLDER	1	HORSES	40
HOLDERS	1	HORSIE	1
HOLDING	42	HOSE	4
HOLDS	10	HOSES	2
HOLE	84	HOSPITAL	52
HOLES	37	HOST	2
HOLIDAY	3	HOT	172
HOLIDAYS	1	HOTDOGS	2
HOLLAND	1	HOTEL	4
HOLLERED	6	HOTELS	2
HOLLERING	1	HOTROD	1
HOLLERS	1	HOUR	26
HOLLOW	2	HOURS	5
HOLLY	10	HOUSE	736
HOLLY'S	2	HOUSES	117
HOLLYWOOD	1	HOW	379
HOLOCAUST	1	HOW'D	2
HOME	540	HOWARD	4
HOMESTEAD	3	HOWDY	12
HOMEWORK	2	HOWE	1
HONESTY	1	HOWEVER	3
HONEY	26	HOWS*	1
HONEYCOMBS	1	HUFF	18
HONEYMOON	4	HUFFED	11
HONG	1	HUFFING	1
HOOD	44	HUFFS	1
HOOK	17	HUG	6
HOOK'S	1	HUGE	6
HOOKED	16	HUGGA	1
HOOKEY	1	HUGGING	2

WORD	FREQ.	WORD	FREQ.
HULA	7	IMAGINATION	1
HULK	2	IMPERIAL	1
HUM	4	IMPORTANT	1
HUMAN	4	IN	3710
HUMANS	3	INCH	4
HUMPTY	17	INCHES	12
HUNDRED	75	INCLUDING	1
HUNDREDS	6	INDIAN	12
HUNGRIER	1	INDIANA	8
HUNGRY	23	INDIANA'S	1
HUNK	2	INDIANAPOLIS	6
HUNSAKER	1	INDIANS	17
HUNT	3	INDIVISIBLE	1
HUNTER	4	INFECTION	2
HUNTERS	1	INITIALS	1
HUNTING	11	INJURED	1
HUNTS	1	INN	1
HUP	4	INNER	1
HURLS	1	INNING	5
HURRICANE	1	INNINGS	1
HURRIED	3	INSIDE	63
HURRIES	1	INSTEAD	30
HURRY	19	INSTRUCTOR	1
HURT	89	INSURANCE	3
HURTING	7	INTEREST	3
HURTS	17	INTERESTING	17
HUSBAND	9	INTERRUPTION	1
HUSBAND'S	1	INTERSECTION	1
HUSH	1	INTO	280
HUSKER	2	INTRODUCE	1
HUT	11	INTRODUCING	4
HUTCH	17	INVENTED	1
HYDRANT	1	INVESTIGATION	2
I	8036	INVISIBLE	11
I'D	22	INVITATION	2
I'LL	204	INVITE	2
I'M	610	INVITED	9
I'S	1	IRIS	1
I'VE	65	IRISH	1
ICE	239	IRON	1
ICES	2	IRONMAN	3
ICICLES	1	IS	1464
ICING	4	ISLAND	39
ICKY	3	ISLANDS	1
IDEA	8	ISLE	1
IDENTITY	3	ISN'T	34
IF	1304	ISRAEL	2
IGNORE	1	IT	6303
ILL	3	IT'LL	15
ILLINOIS	5	IT'S	835

WORD	FREQ.	WORD	FREQ.
ITALIAN	1	JELLY	12
ITCHING	1	JENNIFER	4
ITCHY	1	JENNY	4
ITS	430	JENNY'S	1
ITSELF	1	JERK	1
IVY	1	JERKED	1
J	7	JERRY	16
JACK	37	JESSICA	1
JACK-O-LANTERN	3	JESSIE	4
JACK-O-LANTERN'S	1	JESUS	6
JACKET	8	JET	3
JACKETS	3	JEWISH	3
JACKIE	5	JILL	18
JACKPOT	2	JIM	13
JACKS	2	JIM'S	2
JACKY	4	JIMMY	9
JACOB	2	JIMMY'S	2
JAIL	117	JIMONY	1
JAILS	2	JINGLE	1
JAM	2	JJ	1
JAMBOREE	1	JJ'S	1
JAMES	7	JO	1
JAMIE	33	JOB	8
JAMIE'S	1	JODI	5
JAN	1	JOE	13
JANE	5	JOEY	18
JANET	4	JOHN	21
JANIE	1	JOHN'S	4
JANUARY	3	JOHNNY	13
JAPANESE	1	JOHNNY'S	1
JAR	6	JOHNSON	2
JARS	1	JOHNSONS	1
JASON	22	JOHNSTON	1
JASON'S	2	JOIN	2
JASONS	1	JOINED	3
JAWS	7	JOKE	5
JAY	11	JOKER	24
JEALOUS	1	JOKER'S	2
JEAN	1	JOKERS	1
JEANNIE	2	JOKES	11
JEANNIE'S	1	JOLLY	1
JEANS	3	JONES	5
JEB	1	JONES'	1
JED	4	JOSH	1
JED'S	2	JOY	1
JEEP	7	JOYCE	1
JEFF	26	JUDO	1
JEFF'S	1	JUDY	3
JEKYLL	1	JUGGLERS	1
JELLO	2	JUGS	1

WORD	FREQ.	WORD	FREQ.
JUICE	6	KEY	11
JULIE	3	KEYS	2
JULY	1	KICK	63
JUMP	131	KICKBALL	25
JUMPED	135	KICKED	38
JUMPER	1	KICKER	1
JUMPING	21	KICKING	7
JUMPS	34	KICKOFFS	1
JUNCTION	1	KICKS	16
JUNE	6	KID	74
JUNE'S	1	KID'S	7
JUNGLE	2	KIDDIE	4
JUNGLE'S	1	KIDDING	3
JUNIOR	11	KIDNAPPED	3
JUNK	19	KIDNAPPERS	1
JUNKS	1	KIDNAPPING	1
JUST	1032	KIDNEY	1
JUSTIN	1	KIDS	132
K	5	KIKI	3
KANABLE	1	KIKI'S	1
KANGAROO	8	KILEY	5
KANGAROO'S	1	KILL	42
KANSAS	1	KILLED	42
KARATE	7	KILLER	3
KAREN	12	KILLING	3
KATE	6	KILLS	6
KATE'S	1	KIM	18
KATHLEENA	1	KIM'S	2
KATHY	12	KIMBERLY	7
KAY	4	KIND	212
KAYAKS	1	KINDERGARTEN	48
KEARNEY	3	KINDS	73
KEARNEY'S	1	KING	76
KEEP	140	KING'S	19
KEEPED*	4	KINGED	2
KEEPER	4	KINGS	16
KEEPERS	1	KISS	7
KEEPING	2	KISSED	7
KEEPS	34	KISSES	4
KEITH	4	KISSING	8
KELLY	16	KIT	2
KELLY'S	2	KITCHEN	36
KEN	9	KITE	2
KENDRA	1	KITTEN	10
KENOBI	2	KITTENS	3
KENTUCKY	11	KITTY	9
KEPT	114	KITTY'S	1
KERMIT	2	KLEENEX	2
KETCHUP	4	KNEE	12
KEVIN	1	KNEES	6

WORD	FREQ.	WORD	FREQ.
KNEW	42	LASERS	1
KNIEVEL	13	LASSIE	8
KNIFE	16	LASSIE'S	2
KNIFES	1	LASSO	1
KNIGHTS	2	LASSOED	1
KNIVES	1	LAST	243
KNOCK	52	LASTS	1
KNOCKED	98	LATE	22
KNOCKING	9	LATELY	3
KNOCKS	13	LATER	13
KNOT	2	LAUGH	17
KNOTS	2	LAUGHED	17
KNOW	1823	LAUGHING	48
KNOWS	19	LAUGHS	3
KOALA	1	LAUNDROMAT	4
KOJAK	1	LAUNDRY	3
KOKOMO	23	LAURA	10
KONG	33	LAURA'S	2
KONG'S	1	LAURIE	11
KOOL-AID	1	LAURIE'S	2
KOOTCHIE	2	LAVA	2
KOREAN	1	LAVERNE	4
KRYPTONITE	7	LAVERTY	1
KYGER	2	LAW	2
L	7	LAWN	3
LABORATORY	1	LAWYER	1
LABRADOR	1	LAY	41
LACY	8	LAYING	38
LAD	3	LAYS	8
LADDER	18	LAZY	2
LADDERS	8	LEAD	3
LADIES	8	LEADED	1
LADY	58	LEADER	4
LADY'S	4	LEADS	3
LAFAYETTE	3	LEAF	3
LAID	49	LEAFS	2
LAKE	51	LEAGUE	6
LAMB	1	LEAKED	1
LAMP	6	LEAKING	1
LAMPS	4	LEAKS	2
LAND	89	LEAN	4
LANDED	34	LEANED	1
LANDING	6	LEANING	3
LANDS	19	LEARN	24
LANDSLIDE	1	LEARNED	20
LANE	1	LEARNING	8
LAP	5	LEASH	4
LARGE	3	LEAST	8
LARRY	3	LEAVE	36
LASER	1	LEAVED*	3

WORD	FREQ.	WORD	FREQ.
LEAVES	70	LIGHTER	1
LEAVING	3	LIGHTNING	7
LED	2	LIGHTS	18
LEDERLE	1	LIKE	2314
LEDGE	3	LIKED	45
LEE	6	LIKES	73
LEFT	77	LIKING	1
LEFTOVER	2	LILY	4
LEG	40	LIMBERLOST	1
LEGAL	2	LIMBS	2
LEGO'S	1	LIMIT	1
LEGOS	3	LINCOLN	3
LEGS	33	LINDA	10
LEIA	2	LINE	50
LEIFIE	1	LINED	1
LEMON	3	LINES	18
LENNY	2	LINING	1
LEOPARDS	2	LINK	7
LESS	2	LINUS	1
LESSON	1	LION	39
LESSONS	11	LIONEL	1
LET	236	LIONS	24
LET'S	113	LIP	7
LETS	60	LIP'S	1
LETTER	17	LISA	17
LETTERS	12	LISA'S	4
LETTING	5	LIST	1
LETTUCE	10	LISTEN	18
LEVER	3	LISTENED	5
LEWIS	1	LISTENING	4
LIAR	1	LISTENS	1
LIBBY	1	LIT	4
LIBRARY	13	LITTLE	1181
LICK	19	LITTLER	9
LICKED	7	LITTLEST	9
LICKING	47	LIVE	77
LICKS	4	LIVED	63
LID	6	LIVER	1
LIDS	1	LIVES	50
LIE	2	LIVING	49
LIED	1	LIZARD	11
LIES	1	LIZARDS	2
LIFE	17	LIZZIE	2
LIFEGUARD	1	LOAD	2
LIFT	11	LOADED	4
LIFTED	4	LOAF	2
LIFTS	3	LOBBY	2
LIGAMENT	7	LOBSTER	2
LIGHT	31	LOCK	4
LIGHTED*	3	LOCKED	29

WORD	FREQ.	WORD	FREQ.
LOCKER	4	LUCKILY	2
LOCKS	2	LUCKY	8
LOG	13	LUCY	4
LOGAN'S	6	LUKE	4
LOGGERS	1	LUKE'S	1
LOGS	1	LULLABYE	1
LOLLIPOP	2	LUMP	1
LONDON	1	LUMPS	1
LONE	5	LUMPY	2
LONELY	1	LUNCH	54
LONG	179	LUNCHROOM	1
LONGER	3	LURKEY	1
LONGEST	2	LYING	5
LOOK	209	LYNN	1
LOOKED	115	M	8
LOOKING	71	M'S	1
LOOKOUT	1	MA	2
LOOKS	76	MAC	2
LOOKY	1	MACARONI	6
LOOP	5	MACDONALD	1
LOOPS	3	MACH	3
LOOSE	15	MACHINE	19
LORD	1	MACHINES	3
LORI	6	MAD	53
LORI'S	1	MADDER	1
LOSE	35	MADE	213
LOSED	1	MADED*	2
LOSER	8	MAE	1
LOSERS	2	MAG	1
LOSES	15	MAGAZINE	3
LOST	56	MAGAZINES	1
LOT	224	MAGGIE	1
LOTION	1	MAGIC	18
LOTS	92	MAGNET	1
LOUD	29	MAGNETS	1
LOUDER	2	MAGNIFYING	3
LOUIE	1	MAGOO	4
LOUIS	2	MAID	3
LOUISE	3	MAIL	7
LOUISIANA	1	MAILMAN	1
LOUISVILLE	2	MAIN	2
LOVE	43	MAINE	1
LOVED	7	MAKE	358
LOVES	18	MAKED*	2
LOVING	4	MAKERS	3
LOW	6	MAKES	65
LOWER	5	MAKEUP	3
LOWEST	1	MAKING	49
LUCK	2	MALL	3
LUCKIER	1	MALPH	1

WORD	FREQ.	WORD	FREQ.
MALPH'S	1	MASKED	1
MAMA	211	MASKS	5
MAMA'S	26	MASON	2
MAMMY	1	MASTER	5
MAN	472	MASTERPIECE	1
MAN'S	17	MAT	1
MANAGER	1	MATCH	17
MANAGERS	1	MATCHBOX	1
MANGER	5	MATCHES	7
MANHOLE	1	MATCHING	2
MANNIX	1	MATE	2
MANSION	3	MATH	7
MANTIS	1	MATIC	4
MANY	86	MATINEE	2
MAP	1	MATS	1
MAPLE	1	MATT	3
MAPLECREST	2	MATTER	13
MARBLE	15	MATTHEW	1
MARBLES	36	MATTRESS	4
MARCH	3	MAX	3
MARCHED	1	MAXINE	1
MARCIA	9	MAY	7
MARCO	3	MAYBE	37
MARCY	5	MCBROOMS'S	1
MARDI	4	ME	1195
MARIA	1	ME'S*	1
MARIE	10	MEACHUM	1
MARIE'S	1	MEADOW	3
MARINO	1	MEAL	1
MARK	30	MEAN	173
MARKED	1	MEANEST	1
MARKER	1	MEANESTEST*	1
MARKERS	1	MEANIE	1
MARKET	3	MEANS	30
MARKLAND	3	MEANT	2
MARKS	3	MEASURE	1
MARKY	1	MEASURED	1
MARRIED	26	MEASURING	1
MARRY	2	MEAT	12
MARSH	1	MEATBALLS	1
MARSH'S	1	MEATLOAF	1
MARTIN	1	MEDAL	1
MARTY	6	MEDICINE	5
MARVIN	1	MEDIUM	4
MARX	1	MEDIUM'S	1
MARY	10	MEET	11
MASH	4	MEETED*	1
MASHED	3	MEETING	2
MASHING	1	MEETS	2
MASK	12	MEGALON	2

WORD	FREQ.	WORD	FREQ.
MEGAPUNCH	1	MILLIONS	3
MEGAPUNCHES	1	MILWAUKEE	2
MELODY	1	MIND	7
MELTED	8	MINDS	2
MELTING	11	MINE	107
MELTS	2	MINE'S	12
MEMORIZED	1	MINES	5
MEN	78	MINIBIKE	11
MENACE	4	MINIBIKES	13
MENS*	4	MINIBIKING	1
MEOW	4	MINNESOTA	3
MERRY	8	MINNIE	4
MERRY-GO-ROUND	3	MINNOWS	3
MESS	12	MINUS	1
MESSAGES	1	MINUTE	28
MESSED	8	MINUTES	14
MESSES	3	MIRROR	1
MESSING	2	MIRRORS	1
MESSY	2	MISS	49
MET	18	MISSED	18
METAL	14	MISSES	3
METS	2	MISSING	3
MEXICO	1	MISSION	1
MIAMI	3	MISSIONS	2
MICE	13	MISSISSINEWA	1
MICHAEL	7	MISSOURI	2
MICHELLE	4	MISSY	12
MICHELLE'S	1	MISSY'S	1
MICHIGAN	8	MISTRESS	2
MICK	1	MISTY	1
MICKEY	56	MITCHELL	2
MICROPHONE	9	MITT	11
MID	2	MITTENS	3
MIDAS	1	MIX	9
MIDDLE	101	MIXED	4
MIDNIGHT	6	MIXER	2
MIDNIGHTS	5	MO	4
MIGHT	85	MOBY	4
MIGHTY	3	MODEL	3
MIKE	19	MODELS	6
MIKE'S	1	MOLLY	2
MIKEY	5	MOM	434
MILE	3	MOM'S	34
MILEAGE	1	MOMMIES	90
MILES	5	MOMMY'S	15
MILK	41	MOMO	1
MILKED	1	MOMS	3
MILL	12	MONDAY	5
MILLER	3	MONEY	116
MILLION	30	MONICA	1

WORD	FREQ.	WORD	FREQ.
MONKEY	45	MOVIES	26
MONKEYS	22	MOVING	14
MONOPOLY	33	MOW	2
MONORAIL	4	MOWER	2
MONSON	2	MR.	160
MONSTER	97	MRS.	69
MONSTER'S	3	MS.	5
MONSTERS	32	MUCH	126
MONTH	5	MUD	16
MONTHS	7	MUDDY	2
MONTICELLO	1	MUFFET	10
MOOD	3	MUFFLER	1
MOON	10	MUFFLERS	1
MOORE	1	MUGGS	2
MOORING	1	MUMBLE	1·
MOOSE	2	MUMMIES	1
MOP	2	MUMMY	7
MOPPING	1	MUMPS	1
MORE	389	MUNSTER	1
MORNING	68	MUPPET	2
MORNINGS	5	MUPPETS	2
MORTON	2	MUSCADREO	1
MOSES	2	MUSCLES	2
MOSEY	1	MUSEUM	8
MOST	67	MUSH	2
MOSTEST*	8	MUSHROOMS	4
MOSTLY	17	MUSHY	1
MOTEL	7	MUSIC	16
MOTELS	4	MUST	20
MOTHER	231	MUSTACHE	1
MOTHER'S	32	MUSTARD	1
MOTHERS	9	MUTT	1
MOTHS	1	MUTUAL	1
MOTOR	11	MY	3181
MOTORBOAT	1	MYSELF	19
MOTORCYCLE	24	MYSTERIES	1
MOUNTAIN	18	MYSTERIOUS	1
MOUNTAINS	18	MYSTERY	3
MOUNTIE	2	MYTH	1
MOUSE	113	MYTHS	2
MOUSE'S	1	N	5
MOUSEKETEER	1	NAIL	3
MOUSES*	1	NAILS	2
MOUTH	59	NAME	237
MOUTH'S	1	NAME'S	18
MOUTHS	2	NAMED	84
MOVE	144	NAMES	41
MOVED	26	NANCY	3
MOVES	11	NAP	4
MOVIE	47	NAPKIN	1

WORD	FREQ.	WORD	FREQ.
NAPS	2	NICKNAMES	1
NASTY	9	NICKY	9
NAT	19	NIECE	1
NATHAN	3	NIGHT	200
NATIONAL	1	NIGHT'S	1
NATIVES	1	NIGHTGOWN	1
NATURALLY	1	NIGHTS	6
NATURE	2	NIMBLE	1
NAUGHTY	5	NINA	2
NEAR	11	NINE	60
NEAREST	3	NINES	5
NEARLY	1	NINETEEN	13
NEAT	30	NINETEENTH	1
NECK	17	NINETY	6
NECKLACE	3	NINTH	4
NECKLACES	1	NIP	1
NECKS	3	NO	789
NEED	51	NOBODY	72
NEEDED	8	NOBODY'S	2
NEEDLE	1	NOISE	15
NEEDLES	2	NOISES	5
NEEDS	4	NOISY	3
NEIGHBOR	11	NONE	33
NEIGHBOR'S	4	NONNIE	1
NEIGHBORHOOD	3	NONSENSE	6
NEIGHBORS	3	NOODLES	1
NEIL	1	NOON	4
NEITHER	8	NOPE	56
NERF	2	NORFEL	1
NESS	1	NORTH	5
NEST	14	NORTHWESTERN	1
NESTS	1	NOSE	41
NET	9	NOSED	5
NETS	4	NOSEY	2
NEVER	142	NOT	485
NEW	90	NOTE	9
NEWEST	2	NOTES	4
NEWS	15	NOTHING	168
NEWSPAPER	3	NOTHING'S	2
NEWSPAPERS	1	NOTHINGS	1
NEWTON	2	NOTICE	2
NEXT	170	NOTICED	2
NIBBLED	1	NOVA	1
NICE	87	NOVEMBER	6
NICELY	1	NOW	287
NICER	1	NOWHERE	1
NICKEL	1	NUEVE	1
NICKELS	1	NUMBER	77
NICKLE	1	NUMBER'S	1
NICKNAME	1	NUMBERED	1

WORD	FREQ.	WORD	FREQ.
NUMBERS	24	OPPOSITE	1
NURSE	6	OR	623
NURSERY	3	ORANGE	38
NURSING	3	ORANGES	5
NUT	3	ORDER	1
NUTS	6	ORDERS	1
O	27	ORGAN	1
O'CLOCK	41	OSCAR	5
O'S	2	OSTMAN'S	1
OATMEAL	2	OSTRICH	1
OCEAN	15	OTHER	689
OCHO	1	OTHER'S	10
OCTOBER	3	OTHERS	16
OCTOPUS	4	OTTO	2
OCTOPUSES	1	OUCH	14
OF	2585	OUGHT	3
OFF	470	OUR	357
OFFICE	15	OURS	6
OFFS	2	OURSELF*	5
OFTEN	6	OURSELVES	7
OH	406	OUT	1424
OHIO	1	OUTDOOR	1
OIL	18	OUTDOORS	4
OK	157	OUTFIELD	5
OLD	170	OUTFIELDER	3
OLDER	22	OUTFIT	5
OLDEST	5	OUTLINE	1
OLDS	2	OUTS	7
OLIVE	20	OUTSIDE	119
OLIVIA	1	OUTSIDE'S	1
OLYMPIA	1	OVEN	14
OMAHA	1	OVER	668
OMELET	1	OVERNIGHT	10
ON	3213	OWE	2
ONCE	280	OWL	7
ONE	2522	OWN	54
ONE'S	88	OWNED	3
ONES	102	OWNER	5
ONLY	310	OWNS	2
ONTO	10	OX	8
OOPS	1	OXYGEN	2
OPEN	81	OZ	17
OPENED	43	P	17
OPENER	1	PACK	7
OPENING	5	PACKERS	1
OPENS	9	PACKING	2
OPERATE	2	PACKS	4
OPERATION	9	PAD	8
OPIE	4	PADDLE	10
OPPONENT	2	PADDLES	2

WORD	FREQ.	WORD	FREQ.
PADS	5	PARKER'S	1
PAGE	21	PARKING	2
PAGE'S	1	PARKS	1
PAGES	7	PARLOR	1
PAIL	6	PARROT	4
PAIN	2	PARROTS	3
PAINT	44	PART	111
PAINTBRUSH	2	PART'S	1
PAINTED	14	PARTICULAR	1
PAINTING	19	PARTIES	3
PAINTINGS	2	PARTLY	3
PAINTS	5	PARTNER	6
PAIR	3	PARTNER'S	1
PAIRS	5	PARTNERS	4
PAJAMAS	5	PARTRIDGE	11
PAL	4	PARTS	10
PALACE	3	PARTY	39
PALS	2	PASQUALLE'S	1
PAM	1	PASS	32
PAM'S	1	PASSAGE	1
PAMMY	3	PASSED	6
PAMPA	2	PASSENGERS	1
PAMPA'S	1	PASSES	2
PAMPAS	1	PASSING	4
PAN	12	PASSWORD	2
PAN'S	1	PAST	27
PANAMA	1	PASTE	13
PANCAKES	5	PASTING	1
PANDAS	1	PASTOR	1
PANE	1	PAT	2
PANS	2	PAT'S	1
PANTHER	15	PATCH	15
PANTS	25	PATCHES	3
PAPA	156	PATH	5
PAPA'S	15	PATHS	1
PAPAYA	1	PATROL	102
PAPER	61	PATROLLING	1
PAPERS	22	PATROLS	27
PAPILLON	2	PATTED	1
PARACHUTE	5	PATTERN	1
PARADE	8	PATTING	1
PARADES	3	PATTY	16
PARCHISI	1	PATTY'S	1
PARDELL	1	PAUL	15
PARENT	1	PAUL'S	4
PARENTS	3	PAULMAN'S	1
PARK	61	PAVILLION	2
PARK'S	2	PAW	1
PARKED	1	PAWNS	1
PARKER	1	PAWS	5

WORD	FREQ.	WORD	FREQ.
PAY	38	PET	14
PAYDAY	10	PETALS	1
PAYMENTS	1	PETE	3
PEA	3	PETE'S	1
PEACE	1	PETER	27
PEACOCK	1	PETRY	1
PEACOCKS	1	PETS	14
PEANUT	16	PETTING	2
PEANUTS	4	PHANTOM	2
PEAR	1	PHIL	1
PEAS	3	PHILIPPINE	5
PEBBLES	4	PHILLIP	6
PECK	1	PHONE	15
PECKED	2	PHONE'S	1
PECKING	1	PIANO	3
PECKS	1	PICK	137
PEDAL	5	PICKED	59
PEDALS	2	PICKING	15
PEEK	1	PICKS	10
PEEKED	3	PICKUP	1
PEG	2	PICNIC	8
PEGGY	5	PICNICKING	1
PEGS	6	PICNICS	2
PELICAN	1	PICTURE	63
PEN	3	PICTURES	56
PENALTIES	1	PIE	9
PENALTY	1	PIECE	35
PENCIL	8	PIECES	30
PENCILS	9	PIER	2
PENGUIN	13	PIES	3
PENNIES	1	PIG	119
PENNSYLVANIA	4	PIG'S	5
PENNY	2	PIGEON	4
PENNY'S	2	PIGGIES	12
PENS	3	PIGGY	15
PEOPLE	410	PIGLET	5
PEOPLE'S	6	PIGS	60
PEOPLES	4	PILE	18
PEPE	1	PILED	4
PEPPER	5	PILES	1
PEPPERMINT	15	PILGRIMS	2
PEPPERS	1	PILLOW	11
PER	1	PILLOWS	5
PERFUME	2	PILLS	1
PERFUMES	1	PIN	9
PERRY	2	PINBALL	2
PERSON	212	PINCH	5
PERSON'S	24	PINCHING	1
PERSONS	7	PINE	1
PERU	1	PINEAPPLE	1

WORD	FREQ.	WORD	FREQ.
PING	3	PLAYFUL	1
PING-PONG	8	PLAYGROUND	10
PINGBALL*	1	PLAYING	207
PINK	33	PLAYMATE	2
PINKY	3	PLAYPEN	1
PINNED	3	PLAYROOM	7
PINOCCHIO	15	PLAYS	45
PINOPLY*	2	PLAYTIME	1
PINS	2	PLEASE	24
PINTS	2	PLEDGE	1
PIPE	7	PLEEZERS*	2
PIPES	2	PLOP	1
PIRATES	2	PLUG	6
PISTOL	2	PLUMB	1
PISTOLS	3	PLUMBING	2
PITCH	6	PLUNGER	1
PITCHER	17	PLUNK	1
PITCHER'S	1	PLUNKED*	1
PITCHERS	1	PLUS	11
PITCHES	3	PLUSES	3
PITCHING	3	PLUTO	10
PITTSBURGH	1	PLUTOS	1
PIXIE	5	PLYMOUTH	1
PIZZA	15	POCKET	15
PIZZAS	2	POCKETBOOK	1
PLA-DOH	1	POCKETFUL	1
PLACE	147	POCKETKNIFE	3
PLACES	31	POCKETS	5
PLAIN	8	POEM	3
PLAINTS	2	POEMS	1
PLAN	4	POG	1
PLANE	23	POHLMAN	1
PLANES	5	POHLMAN'S	2
PLANET	16	POINT	48
PLANETARIUM	1	POINTED	2
PLANNED	1	POINTING	1
PLANS	2	POINTS	17
PLANT	8	POINTY	1
PLANTED	2	POISON	9
PLANTS	3	POKE	2
PLASTIC	27	POKED	1
PLATE	11	POKER	1
PLATEFUL	1	POLAR	4
PLATES	4	POLE	29
PLATTER	1	POLES	2
PLAY	777	POLICE	62
PLAY'S	1	POLICEMAN	17
PLAYED	127	POLICEMAN'S	1
PLAYER	14	POLICEMEN	6
PLAYERS	10	POLICEMEN'S	1

WORD	FREQ.	WORD	FREQ.
POLICES*	2	POTS	2
POLLY	4	POTSIE	4
POLO	3	POTTERY	2
POM	1	POTTIES	1
POMS	1	POUND	9
POND	11	POUNDING	3
PONG	2	POUNDS	1
PONIES	5	POUR	11
PONTIAC	1	POURED	2
PONTOON	1	POURING	2
PONY	12	POURS	1
PONY'S	1	POW	9
PONYTAIL	2	POWDER	2
POOCHIE	1	POWER	4
POODLE	3	POWERS	1
POOF	2	POX	2
POOH	26	PRACTICALLY	3
POOH'S	1	PRACTICE	12
POOL	83	PRACTICED	1
POOLS	1	PRACTICING	6
POOP	1	PRAIRIE	2
POOPED	1	PRAY	1
POOR	15	PRAYED	1
POP	29	PRAYING	1
POP'S	1	PREACH	1
POPCORN	13	PREGNANT	3
POPEYE	81	PRESENT	14
POPEYE'S	2	PRESENTS	19
POPPED	14	PRESLEY	8
POPPING	2	PRESS	11
POPS	7	PRESTON	2
POPSICLE	1	PRETEND	39
POPSICLES	4	PRETENDED	8
PORCH	13	PRETENDING	1
PORCHES	4	PRETENDS	3
PORCUPINE	2	PRETTIER	1
PORKY	22	PRETTIEST	1
PORRIDGE	227	PRETTY	56
PORRIDGES	2	PRETZEL	2
PORTABLE	1	PRETZELS	1
POSIES	3	PREVIEW	1
POSITION	1	PREVIEWS	2
POSSUM'S	2	PRICE	2
POST	4	PRINCE	3
POSTER	1	PRINCES	2
POSTMAN	1	PRINCESS	6
POSTS	2	PRINCESS'	1
POT	25	PRINCESSES	1
POTATO	19	PRINCIPAL	2
POTATOES	9	PRINGLE	1

WORD	FREQ.	WORD	FREQ.
PRINTS	2	PUPPET	9
PRISON	3	PUPPETS	12
PRISONER	1	PUPPIES	8
PRIVACY	2	PUPPY	29
PRIVATE	1	PUPPY'S	1
PRIZE	32	PURDUE	3
PRIZES	8	PURPLE	14
PROBABLY	62	PURPLES	1
PROBLEM	1	PURSE	5
PRODUCED	1	PUSH	77
PRODUCTION	1	PUSHED	36
PROFESSION	1	PUSHES	5
PROFESSORS	1	PUSHING	12
PROGRAM	14	PUSSY	1
PROGRAMS	3	PUT	811
PROJECTOR	1	PUTS	42
PROMISE	2	PUTTED*	4
PROMISED	4	PUTTING	28
PRONOUNCE	1	PUZZLE	11
PROOF	1	PUZZLE'S	1
PROPELLER	1	PUZZLES	9
PROPERTIES	2	PX	1
PROPERTY	7	Q	1
PROTECT	3	QUACK	4
PROTECTS	1	QUACKY	1
PROUD	2	QUART	1
PUCK	3	QUARTER	8
PUDDING	4	QUARTERBACK	3
PUDDLE	4	QUATRO	1
PUERTO RICO	1	QUEEN	13
PUFF	18	QUEENIE	2
PUFFED	10	QUEENS	1
PUFFING	1	QUEER	4
PUFFS	2	QUESTION	10
PULL	41	QUESTIONS	6
PULLED	41	QUICK	7
PULLING	14	QUICKEST	1
PULLS	4	QUICKLY	2
PUMP	5	QUICKSAND	1
PUMPED	1	QUIET	15
PUMPER	1	QUIETEST	1
PUMPKIN	29	QUIT	47
PUMPKINS	7	QUITE	6
PUMPS	1	QUITS	1
PUNCH	15	QUITTED*	1
PUNCHED	2	QUITTING	1
PUNCHES	2	QUIZ	4
PUNISH	1	QUIZMO	2
PUNISHED	3	R	4
PUP	6	RABBIT	82

WORD	FREQ.	WORD	FREQ.
RABBIT'S	1	RAT	3
RABBITS	12	RATHER	2
RACCOON	8	RATS	1
RACCOONS	3	RATTLESNAKE	6
RACE	38	RATTLING	1
RACED	2	RAW	2
RACER	9	RAY	8
RACER'S	1	RAYLENE	1
RACERS	1	RAYMOND	2
RACES	10	RAYS	3
RACING	12	REACH	6
RACK	2	READ	103
RACKO	2	READER	3
RACOON	3	READERS	1
RADAR	2	READING	38
RADIO	15	READS	13
RADIOS	1	READY	42
RAG	4	REAL	429
RAGGEDY	12	REALLY	248
RAILROAD	5	REAR	2
RAIN	11	REASON	3
RAINBOW	5	REBA	1
RAINED	3	REBECCA	2
RAINER	8	REBEL	1
RAINING	15	REBUILD	1
RAINS	1	RECEIVER	3
RAINY	2	RECESS	10
RAISE	6	RECESSES	3
RAISED	1	RECORD	22
RAKE	7	RECORDED	1
RAKED	1	RECORDER	59
RALLY	2	RECORDERS	1
RALPH	7	RECORDING	7
RAM	1	RECORDS	12
RAMBLING	1	RED	272
RAMP	20	RED-TAIL	5
RAMPARTS	1	RED-TAILED	1
RAMPS	8	RED'S	1
RAN	189	REDDER	2
RANDY	4	REDEYES	1
RANG	4	REDS	13
RANGE	1	REDSKINS	2
RANGER	9	REEL	1
RANGERS	3	REFEREES	2
RANNED*	9	REFRESHMENTS	1
RARE	1	REFRIGERATOR	6
RARELY	1	REFUSE	2
RASCAL	1	REGGIE	2
RASCALS	15	REGULAR	6
RASH	5	REINDEER	4

WORD	FREQ.	WORD	FREQ.
REINDEER'S	2	RICKETY	1
REINDEERS*	3	RICKY	10
REINS	1	RICKY'S	1
RELAX	1	RID	14
RELAXING	1	RIDDLE	1
RELEASE	1	RIDDLER	2
REMEMBER	275	RIDE	136
REMEMBERED	7	RIDED*	10
REMEMBERS	1	RIDER	1
REMIND	1	RIDERS	1
REMO'S	1	RIDES	47
RENA	2	RIDING	90
REPAIR	1	RIFLE	3
REPEATS	1	RIFLEMAN	3
REPORT	19	RIFLES	2
REPORTED	7	RIGHT	658
RERUN	2	RING	39
RERUNS	1	RINGED	1
RESCUE	3	RINGING	1
RESCUED	2	RINGS	11
RESCUERS	1	RINK	1
RESCUES	1	RIP	1
RESCUING	1	RIPE	1
RESERVOIR	3	RIPPED	4
RESPECT	1	RISK	2
RESPONSIBILITY	1	RIVER	12
REST	93	ROAD	44
RESTAURANT	4	ROADRUNNER	14
RESTED	1	ROADS	2
RESTING	1	ROAR	1
RESTROOM	1	ROB	6
RETRIEVER	1	ROBBED	4
REVERSE	7	ROBBER	6
REVERSES	1	ROBBER'S	2
REVIEW	3	ROBBERING*	1
REWARD	1	ROBBERS	16
REX	1	ROBBIE	2
RHINO	6	ROBBING	3
RHINOCEROS	2	ROBBINS	1
RHYME	1	ROBERT	3
RHYMES	3	ROBES	1
RIBBON	1	ROBIN	38
RIBS	1	ROBIN'S	1
RICARDO	3	ROBINSON	1
RICE	2	ROBINSON'S	1
RICH	13	ROBOT	20
RICHARD	1	ROBOT'S	2
RICHIE	4	ROBOTS	19
RICHIE'S	2	ROCK	57
RICK	3	ROCK-A-BYE	2

WORD	FREQ.	WORD	FREQ.
ROCK'EM	2	ROWED	1
ROCKED	5	ROWS	1
ROCKER	1	ROY	10
ROCKET	18	RUB	3
ROCKETS	6	RUBBED	3
ROCKFORD	1	RUBBER	7
ROCKING	7	RUBBLE	2
ROCKS	49	RUBBLES	1
ROCKVILLE	2	RUDOLPH	26
ROCKY	1	RUDY	1
ROD	4	RUFF	4
RODACK	1	RUG	9
RODE	21	RUGS	2
RODEO	2	RUIN	2
ROG	1	RUINED	3
ROGER	9	RULES	5
ROGERS	5	RUMPLESTILTSKIN	6
ROLL	78	RUN	287
ROLLED	17	RUNAWAY	1
ROLLER	38	RUNG	1
ROLLING	9	RUNNED*	23
ROLLS	13	RUNNER	24
ROMAIN	2	RUNNING	104
RONA	1	RUNS	48
ROO	4	RUNWAY	5
ROOF	24	RUSH	12
ROOFING	1	RUSH'S	4
ROOFS	2	RUSSIAVILLE	1
ROOKIES	2	RUST	2
ROOM	176	RYE	2
ROOMS	3	S	10
ROOSTERS	2	SABRINA	2
ROPE	59	SACK	5
ROPED	1	SACKS	1
ROPES	3	SACRED	1
ROSCOE	4	SAD	9
ROSE	1	SADDLE	1
ROSES	5	SADDLES	1
ROSIE	10	SAFARI	1
ROSIES	4	SAFE	16
ROSS	2	SAFETY	2
ROTTEN	3	SAID	1287
ROUGH	9	SAIL	1
ROUGH'S	1	SAILBOAT	2
ROUND	42	SAILBOATS	2
ROUNDED	1	SAILED	2
ROUNDS	2	SAILING	1
ROUTE	2	SAILOR	4
ROVER	3	SAILS	1
ROW	27	SALAD	3

WORD	FREQ.	WORD	FREQ.
SALE	1	SCARY	27
SALT	24	SCATTERED	2
SAM	16	SCATTERS	1
SAM'S	1	SCENES	1
SAME	123	SCHAFER	3
SAMMY	5	SCHEDULE	1
SAN	2	SCHOOL	254
SANCTUARY	1	SCIENCE	5
SAND	13	SCIENTIST	2
SANDALS	2	SCISSORS	2
SANDBOX	2	SCOOBY	17
SANDPILE	1	SCOOBYDOO	20
SANDRA	2	SCOOT	4
SANDS	1	SCOOTED	1
SANDWICH	11	SCOOTER	4
SANDWICHES	12	SCOPE	1
SANDY	5	SCORE	18
SANG	5	SCORED	1
SANTA	27	SCORES	7
SANTA'S	3	SCOTCH	2
SANTY	4	SCOTT	21
SARAH	5	SCOTTS	5
SAT	91	SCOTTY	3
SATURDAY	30	SCOTTY'S	3
SATURDAYS	10	SCOUT	2
SAUCE	5	SCOUTS	1
SAUCERS	1	SCRAMBLE	2
SAVE	8	SCRAMBLER	2
SAVED	14	SCRAP	2
SAVER	2	SCRAPE	4
SAVES	6	SCRAPED	1
SAVING	4	SCRAPER	2
SAW	318	SCRATCH	2
SAWED	1	SCRATCHED	11
SAWFISH	1	SCRATCHES	2
SAWS	1	SCRATCHING	1
SAY	350	SCRATCHY	1
SAYING	42	SCREAM	4
SAYS	315	SCREAMED	3
SCALES	1	SCREAMING	15
SCANNER	1	SCREAMS	5
SCAR	1	SCREEN	2
SCARE	10	SCREW	3
SCARECROW	5	SCREWS	2
SCARECROW'S	2	SCRIBBLE	1
SCARED	70	SCROOGE	2
SCARES	4	SCRUFFY	2
SCARF	6	SCRUNCHED	1
SCARIEST	1	SEA	13
SCARING	4	SEAL	4

WORD	FREQ.	WORD	FREQ.
SEALS	4	SEVENTEENTH	1
SEAN	4	SEVENTH	2
SEARCH	1	SEVENTY	6
SEARS	2	SEWED	4
SEASHORE	2	SEWER	2
SEASICK	2	SEWERS	1
SEAT	34	SEWING	2
SEATS	5	SHACK	1
SEAWEED	1	SHADOW	6
SECOND	61	SHADOWS	1
SECONDS	2	SHAFFER	1
SECRET	16	SHAGGY	1
SECRETS	1	SHAKE	14
SEE	981	SHAKED	2
SEED	4	SHAKES	1
SEEING	13	SHAKEY'S	1
SEEK	50	SHAKING	2
SEEKER	3	SHALL	1
SEEM	2	SHALLOW	1
SEEMS	4	SHAN'T	3
SEEN	61	SHANNA	4
SEES	14	SHANNON	3
SEIZURES	1	SHAPE	4
SELF	3	SHAPED	5
SELL	5	SHAPES	3
SELLED*	1	SHARE	8
SELLING	4	SHARED*	1
SEMI	1	SHARING	8
SEMIS	1	SHARK	12
SEND	9	SHARKS	7
SENDED*	1	SHARON	5
SENDS	3	SHARP	20
SENSE	3	SHARPEN	2
SENSES	2	SHARPENED	1
SENT	11	SHARPENER	1
SEPARATE	1	SHARPER	2
SERGEANT	8	SHAVE	1
SERVES	1	SHAWN	3
SERVING	2	SHAWN'S	1
SES	1	SHAWNEE	4
SESAME	19	SHE	2509
SET	65	SHE'D	10
SETS	14	SHE'LL	14
SETTED*	2	SHE'S	220
SETTER	1	SHEARS	1
SETTING	16	SHED	2
SETTLE	2	SHEEP	5
SEVEN	89	SHEET	5
SEVENS	2	SHEETS	1
SEVENTEEN	10	SHEILA	3

WORD	FREQ.	WORD	FREQ.
SHELF	4	SHOULDERS	8
SHELFS*	1	SHOULDN'T	3
SHELL	7	SHOVE	1
SHELLS	4	SHOVED	3
SHELLY	15	SHOVEL	1
SHELLY'S	2	SHOW	205
SHELVES	2	SHOW-OFF	1
SHEPHERD	4	SHOWED	29
SHEPHERDS	2	SHOWER	4
SHERBET	1	SHOWERS	1
SHERIFF	10	SHOWING	7
SHERRY	11	SHOWS	59
SHIELD	2	SHRINKING	1
SHIELDS	1	SHRUNK	1
SHIFT	1	SHUMAN	4
SHIMMY	6	SHUT	43
SHINES	3	SHUTTED*	1
SHINY	5	SHY	2
SHIP	16	SICK	32
SHIPPER	1	SICKNESS	1
SHIPS	15	SIDE	106
SHIPWRECK	1	SIDES	6
SHIPWRECKED	1	SIDETRACK	2
SHIRLEY	3	SIDEWALK	11
SHIRT	49	SIDEWALKS	2
SHIRTS	6	SIDEWAYS	4
SHOCKED	3	SIETE	1
SHOE	16	SIGHT	3
SHOED	2	SIGMUND	2
SHOER	1	SIGMUNDS	2
SHOES	51	SIGN	20
SHOOK	1	SIGNAL	1
SHOOT	64	SIGNALING	1
SHOOTED*	3	SIGNED	5
SHOOTING	20	SIGNING	1
SHOOTS	19	SIGNS	3
SHOP	10	SILENT	2
SHOPPED	2	SILLIEST	3
SHOPPING	7	SILLS	1
SHORE	4	SILLY	21
SHORT	19	SILVER	13
SHORTCUTS	1	SILVERWARE	2
SHORTER	1	SIMON	8
SHORTY	1	SIMPLE	6
SHORTY'S	1	SINCE	18
SHOT	68	SINCLAIR	1
SHOTGUN	6	SING	30
SHOTS	1	SINGING	13
SHOULD	17	SINGLE	5
SHOULDER	2	SINGS	9

WORD	FREQ.	WORD	FREQ.
SINK	9	SKIRT	1
SINKING	4	SKIRTS	1
SIR	3	SKIS	1
SIREN	3	SKUNK	10
SISSY	2	SKUNK'S	2
SISTER	212	SKUNKS	2
SISTER'S	23	SKY	25
SISTERS	40	SKYWALKER	2
SIT	105	SLAM	3
SITE	1	SLAMMED	2
SITS	12	SLAP	10
SITTED*	1	SLAPPED	5
SITTEN*	3	SLAPPING	1
SITTER	4	SLAPS	1
SITTER'S	1	SLAW	3
SITTERS	3	SLED	6
SITTING	151	SLEDDING	2
SIX	196	SLEDGE	1
SIX'S	1	SLEEP	88
SIXES	2	SLEEPED*	1
SIXTEEN	15	SLEEPING	106
SIXTEENTH	2	SLEEPS	14
SIXTH	10	SLEEPY	8
SIXTY	4	SLEEVE	2
SIZE	13	SLEEVES	1
SIZED	14	SLEIGH	3
SIZZLERS	3	SLEPT	26
SKATE	9	SLICK	4
SKATEBOARD	1	SLICKY*	1
SKATED	2	SLID	10
SKATERS	1	SLIDE	43
SKATES	6	SLIDE'S	1
SKATING	20	SLIDED*	2
SKELETON	10	SLIDES	6
SKELETONS	3	SLIDING	3
SKI	1	SLIME	1
SKID	2	SLIMY	2
SKIDDED	1	SLINGSHOT	2
SKIDDING	4	SLIP	4
SKIES	3	SLIPPED	7
SKIING	5	SLIPPING	2
SKILL	2	SLIPS	2
SKIN	7	SLIT	1
SKINNED	3	SLOBBER	1
SKINNER	1	SLOPPY	1
SKINNY	11	SLOT	1
SKIP	4	SLOW	11
SKIPPED	1	SLOWER	1
SKIPPER	5	SLOWPOKE	1
SKIPS	3	SLUD*	1

WORD	FREQ.	WORD	FREQ.
SLUG*	2	SNEEZE	3
SLUGS	2	SNEEZING	1
SLUMBER	1	SNIFFED	1
SLY	1	SNIFFING	1
SMACK	2	SNIFFS	3
SMACKED	3	SNOOPY	37
SMACKS	2	SNOOPY'S	4
SMALL	32	SNORED	1
SMALLER	3	SNORKEL	2
SMALLEST	1	SNOW	182
SMALLS	1	SNOW'S	1
SMART	10	SNOWBALL	4
SMARTER	2	SNOWBALLS	3
SMARTEST	1	SNOWCONE	2
SMARTY	1	SNOWED	4
SMASH	3	SNOWING	28
SMASHED	11	SNOWMAN	18
SMASHING	2	SNOWMANS*	1
SMASHUP	1	SNOWMOBILE	2
SMEAR	3	SNOWMOBILING	1
SMEARED	3	SNOWS	1
SMEARS	1	SNOWY	4
SMELL	17	SNUCK*	2
SMELLED	7	SNUCKED*	2
SMELLING	74	SNUFFLE-UPAGUS	1
SMELLS	3	SNUGGER*	1
SMELT	1	SO	1093
SMILES	2	SO'S	1
SMILING	22	SOAK	1
SMITH	1	SOAKED	2
SMOKE	12	SOAKING	1
SMOKES	3	SOAP	10
SMOOCHING	1	SOCCER	10
SMOOTH	2	SOCIAL	3
SMOTHER	1	SOCK	3
SMURF	2	SOCKING	1
SMURFS	2	SOCKO	6
SMURPHETTE	1	SOCKS	10
SNAILS	1	SODAS	3
SNAKE	18	SOFT	77
SNAKES	11	SOFTBALL	3
SNAP	2	SOGGY	1
SNAPPED	2	SOLD	4
SNAPPING	1	SOLDIER	5
SNAPS	1	SOLDIER'S	2
SNEAK	5	SOLDIERS	3
SNEAKED	3	SOLES	1
SNEAKING	3	SOLID	2
SNEAKS	4	SOLO	1
SNEAKY	1	SOLVE	2

WORD	FREQ.	WORD	FREQ.
SOLVED	1	SPANKING	6
SOLVER	1	SPANKINGS	1
SOME	821	SPANKS	2
SOMEBODY	308	SPANKY	18
SOMEBODY'S	181	SPANKY'S	1
SOMEBODYS	1	SPANNER	4
SOMEDAY	2	SPARE	2
SOMEDAYS*	1	SPARK	1
SOMEONE	112	SPARKLE	1
SOMEONE'S	44	SPARKS	1
SOMEONES*	2	SPARKY	1
SOMEPLACE	8	SPEAK	4
SOMERSAULT	3	SPEAKED*	2
SOMETHING	418	SPEAKER	1
SOMETHINGS	1	SPEAKERS	1
SOMETIME	22	SPEAKS	1
SOMETIMES	383	SPEAR	1
SOMEWHERE	40	SPECIAL	26
SOMEWHERES*	1	SPECIALS	2
SON	7	SPECTACULAR	1
SONG	24	SPEECH	1
SONGS	11	SPEED	22
SONNY	2	SPEEDING	2
SOON	22	SPEEDOMETER	1
SORE	5	SPEEDS	1
SORES	1	SPEEDWAY	2
SORRY	33	SPELL	8
SORT	29	SPELLED	2
SORTS	1	SPELLING	4
SOUND	18	SPELLS	2
SOUNDED	1	SPELT*	1
SOUNDING	1	SPEND	4
SOUNDLY	1	SPENDED*	2
SOUNDS	6	SPENT	5
SOUP	33	SPICE	1
SOUPY	1	SPIDER	22
SOUR	1	SPIDERMAN	49
SOUTH	7	SPIDERMAN'S	2
SOUVENIR	1	SPIDERS	7
SOX	15	SPIED	1
SPACE	36	SPIKES	1
SPACEMAN	2	SPILL	5
SPACES	16	SPILLED	5
SPACESHIP	2	SPILLING	3
SPACESHIPS	3	SPILLS	1
SPACY	3	SPILT	1
SPAGHETTI	2	SPIN	41
SPANIEL	1	SPINACH	33
SPANK	5	SPINNED*	4
SPANKED	4	SPINNER	17

WORD	FREQ.	WORD	FREQ.
SPINNERS	1	SQUIRRELS	4
SPINNING	9	SQUIRT	4
SPINS	12	SQUIRTED	1
SPIT	4	SQUIRTS	3
SPITTING	2	STABBED	3
SPLASH	7	STACK	11
SPLASHED	6	STACY	7
SPLASHES	1	STADIUM	2
SPLASHING	1	STAGE	5
SPLINTER	1	STAGES	1
SPLIT	2	STAIRS	37
SPLITS	8	STAIRWAY	1
SPOIL	1	STAIRWAYS	1
SPOILED	3	STAKE	1
SPOKE	1	STALKER	2
SPOKES	2	STALLED	1
SPONGE	1	STALLION	1
SPONGES	1	STAMPED	1
SPOOK	5	STAMPING	1
SPOOKY	13	STAND	47
SPOON	8	STANDED*	1
SPOONS	4	STANDING	31
SPORT	11	STANDS	5
SPORTS	15	STAPLE	2
SPOT	19	STAPLED	6
SPOTS	7	STAPLER	1
SPOTTED	1	STAR	36
SPRAINED	1	STARE	1
SPRAY	5	STARED	1
SPRAYED	6	STARING	5
SPRAYS	2	STARS	6
SPREADED*	1	STARSKY	19
SPRING	5	STARSKY'S	1
SPRINGS	4	START	146
SPRINGTIME	1	STARTED	182
SPRITE	1	STARTING	18
SPRUNGED*	1	STARTLED	1
SPUD	5	STARTS	41
SPUN	2	STARVE	1
SPY	2	STATE	8
SQUAD	3	STATES	4
SQUARE	29	STATION	45
SQUARES	18	STATIONS	2
SQUASH	2	STATUE	4
SQUASHED	1	STATUES	2
SQUEAK	3	STAY	110
SQUEAKY	1	STAYED	55
SQUEEZE	3	STAYING	8
SQUEEZED	2	STAYS	15
SQUIRREL	15	STEAK	4

WORD	FREQ.	WORD	FREQ.
STEAL	10	STOOD	3
STEALED*	4	STOOGES	22
STEALING	4	STOOL	4
STEALS	5	STOOLS	1
STEAMED	1	STOP	110
STEEL	11	STOPPED	43
STEELERS	2	STOPPER	1
STEEP	1	STOPPING	4
STEER	3	STOPS	10
STEERING	5	STORE	59
STEERS	1	STORES	5
STEP	22	STORIES	86
STEPHANIE	13	STORM	4
STEPPED	9	STORY	163
STEPPING	3	STOVE	8
STEPS	33	STOVES	1
STEVE	43	STRAIGHT	35
STEVE'S	2	STRANGE	1
STEVEN	3	STRANGERS	1
STEVENS	1	STRAP	2
STEW	5	STRATEGO	6
STICK	63	STRAW	40
STICKED*	5	STRAWBERRIES	2
STICKER	1	STRAWBERRY	2
STICKERS	4	STRAWS	3
STICKING	15	STREAKING	1
STICKS	38	STREAM	2
STICKY	3	STREAMS	1
STILL	129	STREET	80
STING	4	STREETS	4
STINGED*	2	STRETCH	21
STINGER	1	STRETCH'S	1
STINGERS	1	STRIKE	5
STINGY	1	STRIKED*	1
STINKED*	3	STRIKES	4
STINKS	2	STRING	18
STIR	1	STRINGER	1
STITCHES	12	STRINGS	2
STITCHING	1	STRIPE	3
STOCK	1	STRIPED	10
STOCKING	3	STRIPES	4
STOLE	10	STRIPPED	1
STOLED*	7	STROLLER	1
STOLEN	1	STROLLERS	1
STOMACH	20	STRON'S	1
STOMACH'S	1	STRONG	22
STOMPED	1	STRONGER	5
STOMPING	2	STRONGEST	1
STONE	2	STRONS	4
STONES	3	STRUCK	3

WORD	FREQ.	WORD	FREQ.
STRUT	2	SUNK	4
STU	1	SUNS	1
STUB	1	SUNSET	1
STUCK	33	SUNSET'S	1
STUDIED	3	SUNSHINE	2
STUDIES	3	SUPER	18
STUDY	1	SUPERFRIENDS	3
STUDYING	1	SUPERHEROS	1
STUFF	402	SUPERMAN	34
STUFF'S	1	SUPERS	1
STUFFED	7	SUPPER	47
STUFFING	1	SUPPER'S	1
STUFFS	1	SUPPOSE	7
STUMP	1	SUPPOSED	86
STUMPS	1	SURE	31
STUNG	2	SURPRISE	16
STUNK	3	SURPRISED	1
STUPID	10	SURPRISES	5
STURDY	1	SURROUNDED	5
STURGESS	1	SUSAN	14
STYLE	1	SUSPECT	1
SUB	3	SUZY	2
SUBMARINE	4	SWALLOWED	8
SUBS	1	SWALLOWS	1
SUBSTITUTE	1	SWAM	9
SUCH	8	SWAMMED *	2
SUCKED	4	SWAMP	1
SUCKER	3	SWAT	6
SUCKERS	3	SWATTER	4
SUCKING	1	SWEAT	1
SUCTION	1	SWEATER	16
SUDDEN	4	SWEATERS	24
SUDDENLY	3	SWEATING	1
SUE	3	SWEATY	2
SUFFOCATE	2	SWEEP	3
SUGAR	4	SWEEPER	1
SUIT	23	SWEEPING	2
SUITCASE	2	SWEET	11
SUITCASES	1	SWELL	1
SUITS	6	SWELLED	1
SUMMER	38	SWIM	45
SUMMERS	7	SWIMMED*	6
SUMMERTIME	2	SWIMMING	93
SUN	11	SWIMS	3
SUN'S	1	SWING	39
SUNBURNED	2	SWINGED*	2
SUNDAES	1	SWINGING	6
SUNDAY	28	SWINGS	15
SUNDAYS	7	SWIPED	2
SUNFISH	1	SWIRLING	1

WORD	FREQ.	WORD	FREQ.
SWISH	1	TANGLED	2
SWISHED	1	TANGLES	1
SWISS	3	TANK	7
SWITCH	3	TANKS	8
SWITCHED	1	TANYA	13
SWITCHES	2	TAP	22
SWITCHING	1	TAPE	76
SWITCHMAN	1	TAPES	2
SWOLLED*	1	TAPPED	3
SWORD	4	TAPPING	3
SWORDFISH	3	TAPS	3
SWUNG	2	TARDY	1
SYCAMORE	3	TARGET	4
SYLVESTER	1	TARGETS	3
SYRUP	2	TART	1
T	7	TARZAN	3
T-SHIRTS	1	TASK	3
TABLE	50	TASTE	16
TABLES	2	TASTED	67
TABLET	1	TASTES	5
TACKLE	19	TASTING	6
TACKLED	6	TATTLE	2
TACKLES	3	TAUGHT	7
TACKLING	2	TAXES	4
TACO	1	TAXI	1
TACO'S	1	TAXICAB	1
TADPOLE	1	TAYLOR	4
TAG	105	TEA	6
TAGGED	23	TEACH	7
TAGGING	2	TEACHED*	2
TAGS	20	TEACHER	80
TAIL	28	TEACHER'S	7
TAIL'S	1	TEACHERS	3
TAILS	5	TEACHES	2
TAKE	386	TEACHING	1
TAKED*	5	TEAM	93
TAKEN	3	TEAM'S	1
TAKES	65	TEAMS	5
TAKING	41	TEAPOT	2
TALE	5	TEAPOTS	1
TALK	76	TEAR	11
TALKED	16	TEARED*	1
TALKING	45	TEARING	5
TALKS	22	TEARS	6
TALL	17	TEASE	4
TALLER	8	TEASED	1
TAMED	3	TEASING	1
TAMMY	5	TED	3
TAMMY'S	1	TEDDY	4
TAN	3	TEE	3

WORD	FREQ.	WORD	FREQ.
TEENAGER	1	THEM	1509
TEENAGERS	1	THEM'S*	2
TEENSY	4	THEMS*	3
TEENY	4	THEMSELVES	5
TEES	1	THEN	4743
TEETER	3	THERE	1945
TEETH	41	THERE'LL	1
TELEPHONE	13	THERE'S	1152
TELEPHONES	1	THESE	393
TELEVISION	25	THEY	3821
TELL	231	THEY'D	2
TELLED*	4	THEY'LL	29
TELLING	21	THEY'RE	399
TELLS	45	THEY'S*	4
TEN	97	THEY'VE	6
TENDER	4	THICK	1
TENDS	1	THIMBLE	3
TENNESSEE	7	THIN	4
TENNIS	17	THING	587
TENSION	1	THING'S	3
TENT	8	THINGS	407
TENTH	2	THINK	578
TENTS	1	THINKED*	1
TEPEE	1	THINKING	8
TERESA	3	THINKS	14
TERESA'S	1	THIRD	44
TERRIBLE	4	THIRSTY	5
TERRY	6	THIRTEEN	17
TESCADERO	1	THIRTEENTH	1
TEST	5	THIRTY	19
TESTING	3	THIRTY-ONE	1
TESTS	2	THIS	1951
TEXAS	2	THIS-A-WAY	1
THAN	93	THOMPSON	3
THANK	11	THORN	3
THANKING	1	THOSE	189
THANKS	4	THOUGH	74
THANKSGIVING	17	THOUGHT	95
THAT	3125	THOUSAND	17
THAT-A-WAY	5	THOUSANDS	3
THAT'LL	2	THREAD	2
THAT'S	1342	THREATENED	1
THE	11608	THREE	588
THEATER	1	THREES	1
THEATERS	1	THREW	65
THEIR	431	THROAT	5
THEIRS	7	THROUGH	155
THEIRSELF*	1	THROW	114
THEIRSELVES*	1	THROWED*	10
THELMA	3	THROWING	15

WORD	FREQ.	WORD	FREQ.
THROWN	1	TO	6874
THROWS	28	TOAD	2
THUMB	1	TOAD'S	1
THUMP	1	TOADS	1
THUNDER	2	TOAST	4
THUNDERBIRD	1	TODAY	64
THUNDERBOLT	3	TODAY'S	1
THUNK*	1	TODD	5
THURSDAY	7	TOE	12
TIC-TAC-TOE	13	TOENAIL	1
TICK	1	TOES	3
TICKED	16	TOGETHER	77
TICKET	10	TOILET	4
TICKETS	4	TOLD	177
TICKLE	14	TOM	17
TICKLES	8	TOM-TOM	6
TICKLISH	1	TOM'S	1
TICO	1	TOMATO	9
TIDAL	2	TOMATOES	2
TIE	20	TOMB	1
TIED	17	TOMBSTONE	1
TIES	1	TOMMY	7
TIFFANY	3	TOMORROW	19
TIGER	37	TOMORROW'S	1
TIGERS	8	TONGUE	12
TIGGER	6	TONGUE'S	1
TIGGER'S	2	TONGUES	1
TIGHT	10	TONIGHT	22
TIGHTER	1	TONSILS	3
TIGHTROPE	3	TONTO	2
TILL	60	TONY	19
TIM	4	TOO	761
TIME	669	TOOK	340
TIME'S	1	TOOKEN*	4
TIMED	1	TOOL	3
TIMES	101	TOOLS	3
TIMMY	6	TOOTH	17
TIN	5	TOOTHES	1
TINA	5	TOOTSIE	1
TINIEST	1	TOP	118
TINKERBELL	3	TOPPED	1
TINY	7	TOPS	7
TIP	2	TORE	22
TIPPED	2	TORED*	1
TIPPING	1	TORN	3
TIPPY	1	TORNADO	11
TIPS	1	TORNADOES	2
TIRE	13	TORPEDO	1
TIRED	42	TORTURES	1
TIRES	5	TOSS	4

WORD	FREQ.	WORD	FREQ.
TOSSED	1	TRAYS	1
TOTE	1	TREASURE	9
TOTO	4	TREAT	1
TOTTER	2	TREATING	7
TOTTERS	1	TREATS	4
TOUCH	40	TREE	137
TOUCHDOWN	28	TREES	111
TOUCHDOWNS	4	TREK	8
TOUCHED	5	TREK'S	2
TOUCHES	4	TRES	1
TOUCHING	11	TRIALS	1
TOUGH	4	TRICK	14
TOUGHIE	1	TRICKED	5
TOW	2	TRICKS	14
TOWARD	1	TRICKY	1
TOWARDS	1	TRICYCLE	2
TOWEL	2	TRICYCLES	1
TOWELS	2	TRIED	212
TOWER	9	TRIES	50
TOWER'S	2	TRIKE	1
TOWN	21	TRIMMED	3
TOY	17	TRIP	28
TOYS	42	TRIPLE	2
TRACE	1	TRIPPED	9
TRACING	1	TRIPS	4
TRACK	24	TROLL	18
TRACKS	5	TROOP	5
TRACTOR	2	TROOP'S	1
TRACTORS	1	TROPHIES	1
TRACY	12	TROPHY	2
TRACY'S	2	TROPPING	4
TRADE	6	TROT	2
TRADED	1	TROUBLE	50
TRAFFIC	1	TROUBLES	2
TRAIL	5	TROUT	1
TRAILER	27	TROY	9
TRAILERS	5	TRUCK	62
TRAILS	2	TRUCK'S	1
TRAIN	56	TRUCKS	16
TRAINING	3	TRUE	15
TRAINS	14	TRUNK	3
TRAMPOLINE	2	TRUNKS	3
TRAP	13	TRUTH	1
TRAPEZE	1	TRY	242
TRAPPED	10	TRYING	97
TRAPS	9	TTP	1
TRASH	17	TUBE	1
TRAVELING	1	TUBES	2
TRAVIS	1	TUESDAY	4
TRAY	1	TUFFET	6

WORD	FREQ.	WORD	FREQ.
TUGGING	1	TWO'S	1
TUMBLING	5	TWOS	6
TUMMY	7	TY	2
TUNA	1	TYLER	5
TUNE	1	TYLER'S	2
TUNNEL	6	TYPEWRITE	2
TUNNELS	1	TYPEWRITER	1
TUPPERWARE	1	U	8
TURKEY	27	UGLY	12
TURKEYS	3	ULTRA	7
TURN	163	ULTRAMAN	1
TURNED	79	ULTRAMAN'S	1
TURNER	2	UMBRELLA	2
TURNING	9	UMPING	1
TURNS	46	UMPIRE	2
TURTLE	21	UNBUTTONED	1
TURTLES	6	UNCLE	68
TUT	1	UNCLE'S	4
TUT'S	1	UNCLES	2
TUXEDO	3	UNCOMFORTABLE	6
TV	108	UNCOVERED	1
TV'S	1	UNDER	98
TVS	1	UNDERDOG	8
TWEET	6	UNDERGROUND	4
TWEETY	2	UNDERNEATH	9
TWEEZERS	1	UNDERSTAND	1
TWELFTH	1	UNDERWATER	4
TWELVE	37	UNDERWEAR	3
TWENTY	36	UNDONE	1
TWENTY-FIVE	5	UNFORTUNATE	8
TWENTY-FOUR	2	UNFREEZED*	1
TWENTY-ONE	1	UNFROZE	4
TWENTY-SEVEN	2	UNFROZEN	5
TWENTY-SIX	1	UNICORN	8
TWENTY-SIXTH	1	UNICORNS	1
TWENTY-THREE	2	UNIFORM	4
TWENTY-TWO	1	UNIFORMS	1
TWICE	9	UNION	1
TWICEST*	1	UNITED	1
TWIGLEY'S	1	UNIVERSE	1
TWINKIE	3	UNIVERSITY	1
TWINS	8	UNLESS	19
TWIRL	7	UNLOCK	1
TWIRLED	1	UNLOCKED	2
TWIRLER	1	UNLOCKS	3
TWIRLS	2	UNO	7
TWIST	6	UNSTICKED*	1
TWISTED	5	UNTAG*	3
TWISTER	5	UNTAGGED*	1
TWO	687	UNTIE	1

WORD	FREQ.	WORD	FREQ.
UNTIED	4	VOICES	5
UNTIL	106	VOLCANO	2
UP	1799	VOLLEYBALL	6
UPHILL	1	VON	1
UPON	60	VOTE	5
UPSIDE	14	WADE	1
UPSTAIRS	102	WADING	1
UPTOWN	1	WAFFLE	2
US	218	WAFFLE'S	1
USE	70	WAGON	22
USED	84	WAGONS	1
USES	6	WAIT	91
USING	6	WAITED	7
USUAL	1	WAITING	8
USUALLY	36	WAKE	12
UTAH	2	WAKED	1
VACATION	20	WAKES	1
VADER	2	WAKING	5
VALENTINE'S	2	WALK	155
VALENTINES	1	WALKED	45
VALERIE	1	WALKER	1
VALLEY	2	WALKIE-TALKIE	2
VAMPIRE	3	WALKING	85
VAMPIRE'S	1	WALKS	11
VAMPIRES	1	WALL	62
VAN	18	WALLACE	2
VANILLA	5	WALLET	1
VASE	1	WALLPAPER	5
VASELINE	1	WALLPAPER'S	1
VASES	1	WALLS	4
VEGETABLES	4	WALLY	10
VELMA	1	WALRUS	8
VERONICA	3	WALT	12
VERSES	2	WALTER	1
VERSUS	1	WALTONS	2
VERY	103	WANDA	3
VEST	2	WANDERING	1
VET	1	WANT	345
VICTOR	1	WANTED	157
VILLAGE	6	WANTING	4
VINEGAR	2	WANTS	63
VINTON	2	WAR	7
VIPERS	1	WARM	18
VIRGINIA	1	WARMED	1
VISIT	18	WARMER	3
VISITING	5	WARS	14
VISITOR	2	WAS	3275
VISITORS	2	WASH	24
VISITS	2	WASHED	6
VOICE	22	WASHER	1

WORD	FREQ.	WORD	FREQ.
WASHER'S	1	WEEKEND	6
WASHERS	2	WEEKENDS	1
WASHES	1	WEEKS	20
WASHING	9	WEENSY	1
WASHINGTON	5	WEENY	2
WASN'T	133	WEIGH	2
WASP	2	WEIGHT	3
WASTE	3	WEIGHTED	1
WATCH	295	WEIGHTS	1
WATCHED	87	WEIRD	5
WATCHES	3	WEISMILLER	9
WATCHING	51	WELBY	2
WATER	276	WELCOME	7
WATER'S	3	WELFARE	1
WATERED	1	WELL	1057
WATERFALL	3	WENDY	6
WATERFALLS	1	WENT	1777
WATERING	1	WERE	476
WATERMELON	4	WEREN'T	18
WAVE	5	WEREWOLF	3
WAVES	5	WEST	15
WAVING	4	WESTERN	3
WAVY	1	WESTERNS	1
WAX	11	WESTWOOD	1
WAY	326	WET	14
WAYNE	1	WHACK	9
WAYS	14	WHACKED	3
WE	2627	WHALE	12
WE'D	11	WHALES	6
WE'LL	28	WHAM	6
WE'RE	178	WHAT	940
WE'S*	1	WHAT'S	93
WE'VE	17	WHATCHAMACALLIT	2
WEAK	2	WHATEVER	48
WEAPON	1	WHEAT	4
WEAR	74	WHEEL	48
WEARING	37	WHEEL'S	1
WEARS	5	WHEELBARROW	2
WEASELS	3	WHEELER	11
WEATHER	1	WHEELIE	7
WEB	12	WHEELIES	3
WEBBED	3	WHEELS	23
WEBS	21	WHEN	1363
WEDDING	7	WHEN'S	1
WEDDLE	3	WHENEVER	44
WEDNESDAY	3	WHERE	346
WEE	9	WHERE'D	1
WEED	1	WHERE'S	37
WEEDS	5	WHEREVER	9
WEEK	43	WHEY	3

WORD	FREQ.	WORD	FREQ.
WHICH	59	WING	2
WHIFF	2	WINGS	11
WHILE	62	WINKING	1
WHIP	6	WINNED*	2
WHIPPED	5	WINNER	53
WHIPPING	6	WINNERS	3
WHIPPINGS	1	WINNIE	25
WHIPS	9	WINNING	7
WHIRLYBIRD	1	WINS	81
WHISKERS	1	WINTER	37
WHISKEY	3	WIPE	4
WHISPERED	2	WIPED	6
WHISTLE	9	WIPERS	1
WHISTLED	3	WIPING	1
WHISTLES	1	WIRE	7
WHISTLING	1	WIRES	17
WHITE	132	WISCONSIN	1
WHITE'S	1	WISE	2
WHITISH	2	WISH	20
WHO	176	WISHED	1
WHO'S	59	WISHES	4
WHOEVER	145	WISHING	5
WHOEVER'S	3	WIT	1
WHOLE	156	WITCH	79
WHOOP	2	WITCH'S	2
WHOSE	11	WITCHES	7
WHY	105	WITH	1140
WHY'D	1	WITHOUT	37
WICKED	7	WIVES	1
WIDE	6	WIZARD	19
WIDOW	2	WOKE	53
WIFE	21	WOKED	1
WIFES*	2	WOLF	150
WIGGLEY	3	WOLF'S	1
WIGS	2	WOLFMAN	2
WILD	33	WOLFS*	4
WILDCAT	1	WOLVES	1
WILL	146	WOMAN	67
WILLIAM	3	WOMAN'S	1
WILLIAMSON	2	WOMANS	1
WILMA	9	WOMEN	2
WIN	156	WOMENS*	1
WIND	15	WON	77
WINDING	2	WON'T	124
WINDOW	135	WONDER	26
WINDOW'S	1	WONDERED	2
WINDOWS	35	WONDERING	1
WINDPIPE	1	WONDERLAND	1
WINDY	1	WONDERWOMAN	1
WINE	1	WONNED*	1

WORD	FREQ.	WORD	FREQ.
WOO	3	WROTE	15
WOOD	35	WUGGY	1
WOODCUTTER	1	X	25
WOODEN	10	X'S	1
WOODPECKER	16	Y	2
WOODS	50	Y'ALL	7
WOODSMAN	1	Y'ALL'S	1
WOODSTOCK	5	YABA	1
WOODY	16	YACKO	2
WOOS	1	YAHTZEE	6
WORD	24	YAHTZEES	2
WORDS	31	YAKS	5
WORE	7	YARD	39
WORED*	1	YARDAGE	1
WORK	96	YEAH	795
WORKBOOK	2	YEAR	70
WORKED	5	YEARS	45
WORKING	20	YELL	4
WORKS	39	YELLED	5
WORLD	26	YELLING	7
WORM	11	YELLOW	95
WORMS	10	YELLOWISH	1
WORRIED	1	YELLOWSTONE	1
WORRY	4	YELLS	3
WORSE	1	YEP	38
WORSER*	2	YES	115
WORST	1	YESTERDAY	49
WORSTEST*	1	YET	64
WORTH	2	YMCA	1
WOULD	238	YOGI	23
WOULDN'T	90	YOGI'S	2
WOUND	1	YOGURT	1
WOW	15	YORK	2
WRAP	2	YOU	5814
WRAPPED	6	YOU'D	9
WRAPPER	2	YOU'LL	32
WRAPPING	2	YOU'RE	256
WRECK	12	YOU'VE	33
WRECKED	12	YOUNG	1
WRECKING	1	YOUNGEST	1
WRECKS	1	YOUR	474
WRENCH	3	YOURS	16
WRESTLING	6	YOURSELF	10
WRIST	2	YUCK	2
WRIT*	1	YUCKY	2
WRITE	18	YUM	2
WRITES	1	YUMMY	1
WRITING	10	YWCA	1
WRITTEN	1	Z	1
WRONG	41	ZACK	2

WORD	FREQ.
ZEBRA	3
ZERO	15
ZERO'S	1
ZEROES	1
ZIMBA	3
ZIP	3
ZIPPED	1
ZIPPING	1
ZOO	22
ZOOM	23
ZOOMED	1
ZOOS	2

Chapter VI

FREQUENCY LISTING OF THE VOCABULARY

THE vocabulary found in this chapter is arranged by frequency of occurrence with the most frequent word, *and*, listed first, the second most frequent word, *the*, listed second, etc. Thus, all words are listed in descending order of occurrence. Next to each word is a percentage of use figure; *and* represents 6.78 percent of the corpus, *the* represents 4.06 percent of the corpus, *I* represents 2.81 percent of the corpus, *to* represents 2.41 percent of the corpus, etc.

Asterisks appearing next to some entries on the word lists indicate that the words are not grammatically correct or standard English words which one would expect to find in a dictionary. In most cases, these words represent invented words, overgeneralizations of verb tenses, or nonexistent pronouns, all of which are quite common in young children's language. A few asterisked words, notably *founded, lighted,* and *slug,* appear to be legitimate words. However, within the context of the language samples, these words, too, were incorrect verb tenses.

WORD	PERCENT	WORD	PERCENT
AND	6.78	BECAUSE	.36
THE	4.06	SEE	.34
I	2.81	WHAT	.33
TO	2.41	GOING	.32
A	2.35	CAN	.31
IT	2.21	HER	.31
YOU	2.03	AT	.30
HE	1.68	IT'S	.29
THEN	1.66	SOME	.29
THEY	1.34	PUT	.28
IN	1.30	YEAH	.28
WAS	1.15	NO	.28
ON	1.12	BACK	.27
MY	1.11	PLAY	.27
THAT	1.09	TOO	.27
GOT	.94	HOUSE	.26
WE	.92	DO	.25
OF	.90	ABOUT	.25
ONE	.88	BIG	.24
SHE	.88	OTHER	.24
LIKE	.81	TWO	.24
ALL	.77	TIME	.23
GET	.72	OVER	.23
THIS	.68	RIGHT	.23
THERE	.68	FOR	.22
GO	.66	OR	.22
KNOW	.64	I'M	.21
UP	.63	CAN'T	.21
WENT	.62	THREE	.21
DON'T	.59	THING	.21
HAVE	.59	CAME	.20
THEM	.53	THINK	.20
IS	.51	HE'S	.19
OUT	.50	HOME	.19
WHEN	.48	HAS	.19
THAT'S	.47	DIDN'T	.18
IF	.46	BEAR	.18
SAID	.45	NOT	.17
DOWN	.43	HERE	.17
BUT	.43	GOES	.17
ME	.42	AROUND	.17
LITTLE	.41	WERE	.17
THERE'S	.40	YOUR	.17
WITH	.40	MAN	.17
SO	.38	OFF	.16
HAD	.38	BABY	.16
HIS	.37	MOM	.15
HIM	.37	THEIR	.15
WELL	.37	ITS	.15
JUST	.36	REAL	.15

WORD	PERCENT	WORD	PERCENT
DAD	.15	RED	.10
BEEN	.15	AGAIN	.09
SOMETHING	.15	ALWAYS	.09
ARE	.15	CHAIR	.09
PEOPLE	.14	YOU'RE	.09
THINGS	.14	FOUR	.09
OH	.14	SCHOOL	.09
STUFF	.14	BY	.09
THEY'RE	.14	REALLY	.09
THESE	.14	LAST	.09
BED	.14	TRY	.08
COME	.14	ICE	.08
DOG	.14	WOULD	.08
MORE	.14	NAME	.08
TAKE	.14	FROM	.08
BE	.13	LET	.08
SOMETIMES	.13	DAY	.08
HOW	.13	MOTHER	.08
GAME	.13	TELL	.08
MAKE	.13	PORRIDGE	.08
OUR	.12	LOT	.08
GIRL	.12	GUY	.08
FIRST	.12	EAT	.08
SAY	.12	SHE'S	.08
GETS	.12	US	.08
BOY	.12	AWAY	.08
WHERE	.12	MADE	.07
WANT	.12	EATING	.07
ANY	.12	KIND	.07
TOOK	.12	PERSON	.07
DID	.12	SISTER	.07
BROTHER	.11	TRIED	.07
WAY	.11	MAMA	.07
SAW	.11	ATE	.07
SAYS	.11	LOOK	.07
ONLY	.11	PLAYING	.07
SOMEBODY	.11	CREAM	.07
WATCH	.10	SHOW	.07
COULD	.10	I'LL	.07
BALL	.10	DOOR	.07
NOW	.10	GOOD	.07
RUN	.10	NIGHT	.07
AFTER	.10	FIVE	.07
HIT	.10	BEARS	.07
ELSE	.10	SIX	.07
INTO	.10	COMES	.07
ONCE	.10	FELL	.07
WATER	.10	EVERY	.07
ANOTHER	.10	BEFORE	.07
REMEMBER	.10	RAN	.07

WORD	PERCENT	WORD	PERCENT
THOSE	.07	MOVE	.05
BEAR'S	.06	HAND	.05
HARD	.06	NEVER	.05
SNOW	.06	CANDY	.05
STARTED	.06	KEEP	.05
SOMEBODY'S	.06	DUCK	.05
LONG	.06	FAVORITE	.05
FLOWERS	.06	BAD	.05
WE'RE	.06	PICK	.05
TOLD	.06	TREE	.05
COULDN'T	.06	BROKE	.05
ROOM	.06	RIDE	.05
WHO	.06	FISH	.05
CATCH	.06	JUMPED	.05
CAR	.06	WINDOW	.05
MEAN	.06	FORGOT	.05
AN	.06	WASN'T	.05
HOT	.06	KIDS	.05
NEXT	.06	WHITE	.05
OLD	.06	CAT	.05
ANYTHING	.06	JUMP	.05
FUN	.06	HI	.05
NOTHING	.06	STILL	.05
HEAD	.06	FRIEND	.04
STORY	.06	BLUE	.04
TURN	.06	FIRE	.04
AS	.06	PLAYED	.04
FUNNY	.06	ALMOST	.04
GUYS	.06	FAST	.04
HEY	.06	FIND	.04
MR.	.06	MUCH	.04
OK	.05	CAUGHT	.04
WANTED	.05	EVEN	.04
PAPA	.05	CARTOONS	.04
WHOLE	.05	DOES	.04
WIN	.05	WON'T	.04
THROUGH	.05	SAME	.04
WALK	.05	OUTSIDE	.04
FORGET	.05	PIG	.04
CARDS	.05	GRANDMA	.04
CALLED	.05	TOP	.04
SITTING	.05	BOOK	.04
CARD	.05	GIVE	.04
WOLF	.05	HOUSES	.04
BLACK	.05	JAIL	.04
PLACE	.05	GAVE	.04
START	.05	MONEY	.04
WILL	.05	FOUND	.04
WHOEVER	.05	LOOKED	.04
END	.05	YES	.04

WORD	PERCENT	WORD	PERCENT
DONE	.04	TEN	.03
GAMES	.04	TRYING	.03
KEPT	.04	EXCEPT	.03
THROW	.04	WORK	.03
LET'S	.04	THOUGHT	.03
MOUSE	.04	YELLOW	.03
AIN'T	.04	DOESN'T	.03
HAIR	.04	BUNNY	.03
HIDE	.04	FOOTBALL	.03
SOMEONE	.04	REST	.03
EVERYBODY	.04	SWIMMING	.03
PART	.04	TEAM	.03
TREES	.04	THAN	.03
EACH	.04	WHAT'S	.03
STAY	.04	EYES	.03
STOP	.04	LOTS	.03
BASEBALL	.04	BOARD	.03
CAUSE	.04	COLOR	.03
GETTING	.04	GIRLS	.03
COMING	.04	SAT	.03
FRIENDS	.04	WAIT	.03
TV	.04	MOMMIES	.03
DADDY	.04	NEW	.03
DIFFERENT	.04	RIDING	.03
MINE	.04	WOULDN'T	.03
DOING	.04	HURT	.03
EVERYTHING	.04	LAND	.03
SIDE	.04	SEVEN	.03
SLEEPING	.04	BETTER	.03
UNTIL	.04	BROWN	.03
BOTH	.04	ONE'S	.03
GOTS*	.04	SLEEP	.03
SIT	.04	GOLDILOCKS	.03
TAG	.04	NICE	.03
WHY	.04	WATCHED	.03
RUNNING	.04	COLD	.03
READ	.04	MANY	.03
VERY	.04	STORIES	.03
ONES	.04	SUPPOSED	.03
PATROL	.04	FATHER	.03
UPSTAIRS	.04	HEARD	.03
BIKE	.04	MIGHT	.03
MIDDLE	.04	WALKING	.03
TIMES	.04	HANDS	.03
CHRISTMAS	.03	HERE'S	.03
BIRTHDAY	.03	HOLE	.03
GREEN	.03	NAMED	.03
KNOCKED	.03	USED	.03
UNDER	.03	BUNCH	.03
MONSTER	.03	DAYS	.03

WORD	PERCENT	WORD	PERCENT
GHOST	.03	LEAVES	.02
POOL	.03	SCARED	.02
BUGS	.03	USE	.02
CALL	.03	YEAR	.02
EVER	.03	ANIMALS	.02
HEAR	.03	BILLY	.02
HELP	.03	HAPPENED	.02
RABBIT	.03	MRS.	.02
OPEN	.03	MORNING	.02
POPEYE	.03	SHOT	.02
WINS	.03	UNCLE	.02
STREET	.03	MOST	.02
TEACHER	.03	TASTED	.02
TURNED	.03	WOMAN	.02
WITCH	.03	BIT	.02
BAT	.03	BUS	.02
MEN	.03	BUY	.02
ROLL	.03	CARS	.02
BOAT	.03	EIGHT	.02
FEET	.03	FIGHT	.02
LEFT	.03	I'VE	.02
LIVE	.03	MAKES	.02
NUMBER	.03	SET	.02
PUSH	.03	TAKES	.02
SOFT	.03	THREW	.02
TOGETHER	.03	SHOOT	.02
WON	.03	TODAY	.02
BIRD	.03	YET	.02
KING	.03	CUT	.02
LOOKS	.03	GROUND	.02
TALK	.03	INSIDE	.02
TAPE	.03	KICK	.02
BASE	.03	LIVED	.02
HUNDRED	.03	PICTURE	.02
FACE	.03	STICK	.02
FOOD	.03	WANTS	.02
KID	.03	POLICE	.02
SMELLING	.03	PROBABLY	.02
THOUGH	.03	TRUCK	.02
WEAR	.03	WALL	.02
DOGS	.03	WHILE	.02
FALL	.03	ACROSS	.02
HIGH	.03	BASKETBALL	.02
KINDS	.03	FOX	.02
LIKES	.03	HALF	.02
NOBODY	.03	PAPER	.02
BEST	.02	PARK	.02
LOOKING	.02	SECOND	.02
BABY'S	.02	SEEN	.02
GRANDMA'S	.02	ALREADY	.02

WORD	PERCENT	WORD	PERCENT
BOYS	.02	KNOCK	.02
DICE	.02	BOUGHT	.02
FISHING	.02	CARTOON	.02
GIANT	.02	LAKE	.02
LETS	.02	NEED	.02
NINE	.02	SHOES	.02
PIGS	.02	WATCHING	.02
TILL	.02	BIGGER	.02
UPON	.02	COUNT	.02
BLOW	.02	DOCTOR	.02
COUSIN	.02	FLY	.02
FOOT	.02	FRONT	.02
MOUTH	.02	LINE	.02
PICKED	.02	LIVES	.02
RECORDER	.02	SEEK	.02
ROPE	.02	TABLE	.02
SHOWS	.02	TRIES	.02
STORE	.02	TROUBLE	.02
WHICH	.02	WOODS	.02
WHO'S	.02	AIR	.02
CHARLIE	.02	BUILD	.02
LADY	.02	CLOSE	.02
AGO	.02	GUESS	.02
ASKED	.02	HELLO	.02
ROCK	.02	LAID	.02
FAR	.02	LIVING	.02
LOST	.02	MAKING	.02
MICKEY	.02	MISS	.02
NOPE	.02	ROCKS	.02
PICTURES	.02	SHIRT	.02
PRETTY	.02	SPIDERMAN	.02
TRAIN	.02	YESTERDAY	.02
BOX	.02	AUNT	.02
DRAW	.02	BROUGHT	.02
GOAT	.02	BUILDING	.02
GREAT	.02	CHICKEN	.02
STAYED	.02	COLORS	.02
ALONG	.02	CONE	.02
CIRCLE	.02	EYE	.02
LUNCH	.02	HAVEN'T	.02
OWN	.02	KINDERGARTEN	.02
CLOTHES	.02	LAUGHING	.02
MAD	.02	POINT	.02
WINNER	.02	RUNS	.02
WOKE	.02	WHATEVER	.02
BEHIND	.02	WHEEL	.02
EITHER	.02	ASK	.02
GONE	.02	BRIDGE	.02
HOLD	.02	BRING	.02
HOSPITAL	.02	DOLLARS	.02

WORD	PERCENT	WORD	PERCENT
LICKING	.02	PUTS	.01
MOVIE	.02	READY	.01
QUIT	.02	ROUND	.01
RIDES	.02	SAYING	.01
STAND	.02	TIRED	.01
SUPPER	.02	TOYS	.01
APPLES	.02	AM	.01
BATMAN	.02	BALLS	.01
BREAK	.02	BEAT	.01
HILL	.02	BLEW	.01
HITS	.02	FAT	.01
HORSE	.02	GODZILLA	.01
TURNS	.02	LAY	.01
BOOKS	.02	MILK	.01
BOTTOM	.02	NAMES	.01
FLOOR	.02	NOSE	.01
GOOSE	.02	O'CLOCK	.01
HE'LL	.02	PULL	.01
LIKED	.02	PULLED	.01
MONKEY	.02	SPIN	.01
PLAYS	.02	STARTS	.01
STATION	.02	TAKING	.01
SWIM	.02	TEETH	.01
TALKING	.02	WRONG	.01
TELLS	.02	DIED	.01
WALKED	.02	FLOWER	.01
YEARS	.02	GRAMMA	.01
ALSO	.02	HELPED	.01
GRASS	.02	HORSES	.01
GUN	.02	LEG	.01
HAVING	.02	SISTERS	.01
HOOD	.02	SOMEWHERE	.01
PAINT	.02	STRAW	.01
ROAD	.02	TOUCH	.01
SOMEONE'S	.02	ASLEEP	.01
THIRD	.02	BIONIC	.01
WHENEVER	.02	BRUTUS	.01
LOVE	.02	DAD'S	.01
OPENED	.02	ISLAND	.01
SHUT	.02	LION	.01
SLIDE	.02	PARTY	.01
STEVE	.02	PRETEND	.01
STOPPED	.02	RING	.01
WEEK	.02	SWING	.01
BROTHERS	.01	WORKS	.01
FIGHTING	.01	YARD	.01
HOLDING	.01	BEDROOM	.01
KILL	.01	COAT	.01
KILLED	.01	DEAD	.01
KNEW	.01	DISHES	.01

WORD	PERCENT	WORD	PERCENT
GRANDPA	.01	BOMB	.01
HAT	.01	BUCKET	.01
KICKED	.01	BUILT	.01
LAYING	.01	CLASS	.01
ORANGE	.01	DOLL	.01
PAY	.01	FROZEN	.01
RACE	.01	ISN'T	.01
READING	.01	JUMPS	.01
ROBIN	.01	KEEPS	.01
ROLLER	.01	LANDED	.01
STICKS	.01	MOM'S	.01
SUMMER	.01	SEAT	.01
YEP	.01	SUPERMAN	.01
BAG	.01	BOOM	.01
BINGO	.01	BOWL	.01
CHIN	.01	COUPLE	.01
GINGERBREAD	.01	DOG'S	.01
HAPPY	.01	DOLLAR	.01
HOLES	.01	FAMILY	.01
JACK	.01	JAMIE	.01
MAYBE	.01	KONG	.01
SNOOPY	.01	LEGS	.01
STAIRS	.01	MONOPOLY	.01
TIGER	.01	NONE	.01
TWELVE	.01	PINK	.01
WEARING	.01	SORRY	.01
WHERE'S	.01	SOUP	.01
WINTER	.01	SPINACH	.01
WITHOUT	.01	STEPS	.01
APPLE	.01	STUCK	.01
BRICKS	.01	WILD	.01
CHAIRS	.01	YOU'VE	.01
FINALLY	.01	BLOOD	.01
KITCHEN	.01	BOZO	.01
LEAVE	.01	CHASE	.01
MARBLES	.01	DRESS	.01
PUSHED	.01	FIELD	.01
SPACE	.01	GYM	.01
STAR	.01	MONSTERS	.01
TWENTY	.01	MOTHER'S	.01
USUALLY	.01	PASS	.01
BUTTON	.01	PRIZE	.01
CHECKERS	.01	SICK	.01
FALLS	,.01	SMALL	.01
GRADE	.01	YOU'LL	.01
LOSE	.01	ANYBODY	.01
PIECE	.01	BABIES	.01
STRAIGHT	.01	CAGE	.01
WINDOWS	.01	CATS	.01
WOOD	.01	COUSINS	.01

WORD	PERCENT	WORD	PERCENT
FASTER	.01	SNOWING	<.01
GUNS	.01	SUNDAY	<.01
LIGHT	.01	TAIL	<.01
PLACES	.01	THROWS	<.01
STANDING	.01	TOUCHDOWN	<.01
SURE	.01	TRIP	<.01
WORDS	.01	WE'LL	<.01
ANIMAL	.01	AGAINST	<.01
BROTHER'S	.01	BIRDS	<.01
CAKE	.01	BUTTONS	<.01
CHRIS	.01	CHIMNEY	<.01
ENOUGH	.01	EMERGENCY	<.01
FIXED	.01	FEED	<.01
INSTEAD	.01	FIFTEEN	<.01
MARK	.01	FINGER	<.01
MEANS	.01	GOAL	<.01
MILLION	.01	GRANDMOTHER	<.01
NEAT	.01	O	<.01
PIECES	.01	PAST	<.01
SATURDAY	.01	PATROLS	<.01
SING	.01	PETER	<.01
BLOWED*	.01	PLASTIC	<.01
DRESSED	.01	ROW	<.01
EATS	.01	SANTA	<.01
HAUNTED	.01	SCARY	<.01
LOCKED	.01	TRAILER	<.01
LOUD	.01	TURKEY	<.01
POLE	.01	ARM	<.01
POP	.01	CAMPING	<.01
PUMPKIN	.01	COW	<.01
PUPPY	.01	DOROTHY	<.01
SHOWED	.01	FIGHTS	<.01
SORT	.01	FLEW	<.01
SQUARE	.01	HIDES	<.01
THEY'LL	.01	HONEY	<.01
AHEAD	<.01	HOUR	<.01
AIRPLANE	<.01	JEFF	<.01
AUSTIN	<.01	MAMA'S	<.01
BANK	<.01	MARRIED	<.01
BITE	<.01	MOVED	<.01
BRIAN	<.01	MOVIES	<.01
CASPER	<.01	POOH	<.01
CLEAN	<.01	RUDOLPH	<.01
CLOSET	<.01	SLEPT	<.01
COASTER	<.01	SPECIAL	<.01
EASY	<.01	WONDER	<.01
FLINTSTONE	<.01	WORLD	<.01
FRIEND'S	<.01	CALLING	<.01
MINUTE	<.01	CAMPER	<.01
PUTTING	<.01	CHASING	<.01

WORD	PERCENT	WORD	PERCENT
CITY	<.01	CORNER	<.01
CLEAR	<.01	DINOSAUR	<.01
CLIMB	<.01	DOWNSTAIRS	<.01
DADDY'S	<.01	DUCKS	<.01
DIRT	<.01	EGG	<.01
FARM	<.01	EGGS	<.01
FLORIDA	<.01	FRIDAY	<.01
GIRLFRIEND	<.01	GOATS	<.01
HARDLY	<.01	GOLD	<.01
KICKBALL	<.01	HEADS	<.01
PANTS	<.01	HEAVY	<.01
POT	<.01	HUNGRY	<.01
SKY	<.01	KOKOMO	<.01
TELEVISION	<.01	PLANE	<.01
WINNIE	<.01	RUNNED*	<.01
X	<.01	SISTER'S	<.01
BACKWARDS	<.01	SUIT	<.01
BIGFOOT	<.01	TAGGED	<.01
BONE	<.01	WHEELS	<.01
CARE	<.01	YOGI	<.01
COOKIE	<.01	ZOOM	<.01
CRYING	<.01	BARS	<.01
DONALD	<.01	BASES	<.01
EM	<.01	BILL	<.01
FIFTY	<.01	BOY'S	<.01
GAS	<.01	CATCHES	<.01
GIRL'S	<.01	CINDERELLA	<.01
GIVES	<.01	CLAUS'S	<.01
JOKER	<.01	COWBOY	<.01
LEARN	<.01	DARK	<.01
LIONS	<.01	DUMB	<.01
MOTORCYCLE	<.01	FEW	<.01
NUMBERS	<.01	FROG	<.01
PERSON'S	<.01	GHOSTS	<.01
PLEASE	<.01	HID	<.01
ROOF	<.01	I'D	<.01
RUNNER	<.01	JASON	<.01
SALT	<.01	LATE	<.01
SONG	<.01	MONKEYS	<.01
SWEATERS	<.01	OLDER	<.01
TRACK	<.01	PAPERS	<.01
WASH	<.01	PORKY	<.01
WORD	<.01	RECORD	<.01
BASEMENT	<.01	SMILING	<.01
BASKET	<.01	SOMETIME	<.01
BEDS	<.01	SOON	<.01
BRADY	<.01	SPEED	<.01
BRICK	<.01	SPIDER	<.01
CHEESE	<.01	STEP	<.01
CHURCH	<.01	STOOGES	<.01

WORD	PERCENT	WORD	PERCENT
STRONG	<.01	FOREST	<.01
TALKS	<.01	FULL	<.01
TAP	<.01	GORILLA	<.01
TONIGHT	<.01	HATE	<.01
TORE	<.01	LEARNED	<.01
VOICE	<.01	MUST	<.01
WAGON	<.01	OLIVE	<.01
ZOO	<.01	RAMP	<.01
ACT	<.01	ROBOT	<.01
ANSWERED	<.01	SCOOBYDOO	<.01
AREN'T	<.01	SHARP	<.01
BARN	<.01	SHOOTING	<.01
BELT	<.01	SIGN	<.01
BOATS	<.01	SKATING	<.01
BOTTLE	<.01	STOMACH	<.01
CHANNEL	<.01	TAGS	<.01
CLOCK	<.01	TIE	<.01
COLORED	<.01	VACATION	<.01
CRAZY	<.01	WEEKS	<.01
DOLLS	<.01	WISH	<.01
DROP	<.01	WORKING	<.01
ELEVEN	<.01	AIRPLANES	<.01
EVERYONE	<.01	ALONE	<.01
FENCE	<.01	ANGELS	<.01
GARAGE	<.01	BEACH	<.01
GLAD	<.01	BEANS	<.01
HANGING	<.01	BET	<.01
JOHN	<.01	BLOCK	<.01
JUMPING	<.01	BOBBY	<.01
PAGE	<.01	BURNED	<.01
RODE	<.01	CAVE	<.01
SCOTT	<.01	CHRISTY	<.01
SILLY	<.01	CLIMBED	<.01
STRETCH	<.01	COOKIES	<.01
TELLING	<.01	CROSS	<.01
TOWN	<.01	DAFFY	<.01
TURTLE	<.01	DONNY	<.01
WEBS	<.01	DRINK	<.01
WIFE	<.01	ELVIS	<.01
ARMS	<.01	FALLING	<.01
BATHROOM	<.01	HALLOWEEN	<.01
BUTTER	<.01	HEART	<.01
CASTLE	<.01	HURRY	<.01
DANDELIONS	<.01	JUNK	<.01
DINNER	<.01	KING'S	<.01
DOGGIE	<.01	KNOWS	<.01
DROPPED	<.01	LANDS	<.01
FIX	<.01	LICK	<.01
FLAG	<.01	MACHINE	<.01
FLYING	<.01	MIKE	<.01

WORD	PERCENT	WORD	PERCENT
MYSELF	<.01	MOUNTAINS	<.01
NAT	<.01	NAME'S	<.01
PAINTING	<.01	OIL	<.01
POTATO	<.01	PILE	<.01
PRESENTS	<.01	PUFF	<.01
REPORT	<.01	ROCKET	<.01
ROBOTS	<.01	SCORE	<.01
SESAME	<.01	SINCE	<.01
SHOOTS	<.01	SNAKE	<.01
SHORT	<.01	SNOWMAN	<.01
SPOT	<.01	SOUND	<.01
STARSKY	<.01	SPANKY	<.01
TACKLE	<.01	SQUARES	<.01
THIRTY	<.01	STARTING	<.01
TOMORROW	<.01	STRING	<.01
TONY	<.01	SUPER	<.01
UNLESS	<.01	TROLL	<.01
WIZARD	<.01	VAN	<.01
AFRAID	<.01	VISIT	<.01
ANDY	<.01	WARM	<.01
ANGIE	<.01	WEREN'T	<.01
APARTMENT	<.01	WRITE	<.01
BEE	<.01	BAR	<.01
BOMBS	<.01	BEEP	<.01
BUILDINGS	<.01	BELL	<.01
CALLS	<.01	CIRCUS	<.01
CHASED	<.01	CLICK	<.01
CHILDREN	<.01	CLOWN	<.01
COUCH	<.01	COMED*	<.01
CRASHED	<.01	DEAR	<.01
DISNEY	<.01	DIRTY	<.01
DROWNED	<.01	FIFTH	<.01
FAIR	<.01	FLAT	<.01
FORTY	<.01	FLIES	<.01
FREE	<.01	FRED	<.01
GREG	<.01	GROW	<.01
HOCKEY	<.01	HOOK	<.01
HUFF	<.01	HUMPTY	<.01
JILL	<.01	HURTS	<.01
JOEY	<.01	HUTCH	<.01
KIM	<.01	INDIANS	<.01
LADDER	<.01	INTERESTING	<.01
LIGHTS	<.01	LAUGH	<.01
LINES	<.01	LAUGHED	<.01
LISTEN	<.01	LETTER	<.01
LOVES	<.01	LIFE	<.01
MAGIC	<.01	LISA	<.01
MET	<.01	MAN'S	<.01
MISSED	<.01	MATCH	<.01
MOUNTAIN	<.01	MOSTLY	<.01

WORD	PERCENT	WORD	PERCENT
NECK	<.01	KELLY	<.01
OZ	<.01	KICKS	<.01
P	<.01	KINGS	<.01
PITCHER	<.01	KNIFE	<.01
POINTS	<.01	MUD	<.01
POLICEMAN	<.01	MUSIC	<.01
ROLLED	<.01	OTHERS	<.01
SCOOBY	<.01	PATTY	<.01
SHOULD	<.01	PEANUT	<.01
SMELL	<.01	PLANET	<.01
SPINNER	<.01	ROBBERS	<.01
TALL	<.01	SAFE	<.01
TENNIS	<.01	SAM	<.01
THANKSGIVING	<.01	SECRET	<.01
THIRTEEN	<.01	SETTING	<.01
THOUSAND	<.01	SHIP	<.01
TIED	<.01	SHOE	<.01
TOM	<.01	SPACES	<.01
TOOTH	<.01	SURPRISE	<.01
TOY	<.01	SWEATER	<.01
TRASH	<.01	TALKED	<.01
WE'VE	<.01	TASTE	<.01
WIRES	<.01	TICKED	<.01
ALFALFA	<.01	TRUCKS	<.01
BANANA	<.01	WOODPECKER	<.01
BARNEY	<.01	WOODY	<.01
BELIEVE	<.01	YOURS	<.01
BOB	<.01	AFTERNOON	<.01
BORN	<.01	ALLIGATOR	<.01
BREAD	<.01	ANN	<.01
BUSTED	<.01	APE	<.01
CIRCLES	<.01	BODY	<.01
CLOSED	<.01	BOUNCE	<.01
CLUB	<.01	BROOM	<.01
COOK	<.01	CASE	<.01
COWBOYS	<.01	CHICKENS	<.01
COWS	<.01	DEEP	<.01
DESK	<.01	DIE	<.01
DOUBLE	<.01	DOO	<.01
DRIVE	<.01	DRIVING	<.01
DUMPTY	<.01	EARLY	<.01
FOLLOW	<.01	FATHER'S	<.01
GLASS	<.01	FINDS	<.01
GOSH	<.01	FORTH	<.01
HEARTS	<.01	GRAMMA'S	<.01
HELPING	<.01	HANG	<.01
HIGHER	<.01	HERS	<.01
HIKE	<.01	IT'LL	<.01
HOOKED	<.01	LOOSE	<.01
JERRY	<.01	LOSES	<.01

WORD	PERCENT	WORD	PERCENT
MARBLE	<.01	COOL	<.01
MOMMY'S	<.01	CRASH	<.01
NEWS	<.01	CURTAINS	<.01
NOISE	<.01	DOORS	<.01
OCEAN	<.01	EARS	<.01
OFFICE	<.01	FARMER	<.01
PANTHER	<.01	FEEL	<.01
PAPA'S	<.01	FERRIS	<.01
PATCH	<.01	FOURTEEN	<.01
PAUL	<.01	HELPS	<.01
PEPPERMINT	<.01	METAL	<.01
PHONE	<.01	MINUTES	<.01
PICKING	<.01	MOVING	<.01
PIGGY	<.01	NEST	<.01
PINOCCHIO	<.01	OUCH	<.01
PIZZA	<.01	OVEN	<.01
POCKET	<.01	PAINTED	<.01
POOR	<.01	PET	<.01
PUNCH	<.01	PETS	<.01
QUIET	<.01	PLAYER	<.01
RADIO	<.01	POPPED	<.01
RAINING	<.01	PRESENT	<.01
RASCALS	<.01	PROGRAM	<.01
SCREAMING	<.01	PULLING	<.01
SHELLY	<.01	PURPLE	<.01
SHIPS	<.01	RID	<.01
SIXTEEN	<.01	ROADRUNNER	<.01
SOX	<.01	SAVED	<.01
SPORTS	<.01	SEES	<.01
SQUIRREL	<.01	SETS	<.01
STAYS	<.01	SHAKE	<.01
STICKING	<.01	SHE'LL	<.01
SWINGS	<.01	SIZED	<.01
THROWING	<.01	SLEEPS	<.01
TRUE	<.01	SUSAN	<.01
WEST	<.01	THINKS	<.01
WIND	<.01	TICKLE	<.01
WOW	<.01	TRAINS	<.01
WROTE	<.01	TRICK	<.01
ZERO	<.01	TRICKS	<.01
ALIVE	<.01	UPSIDE	<.01
AMBULANCE	<.01	WARS	<.01
ARMSTRONG	<.01	WAYS	<.01
B	<.01	WET	<.01
BONES	<.01	ANYWAY	<.01
BROKEN	<.01	APART	<.01
CATCHING	<.01	AWHILE	<.01
CHOCOLATE	<.01	BARREL	<.01
CHOPPED	<.01	BIKES	<.01
CINDY	<.01	BLOCKS	<.01

WORD	PERCENT	WORD	PERCENT
BOA	<.01	SEEING	<.01
BOSS	<.01	SILVER	<.01
BUCKETS	<.01	SINGING	<.01
BURN	<.01	SIZE	<.01
BUTTERFLY	<.01	SPOOKY	<.01
CAMP	<.01	STEPHANIE	<.01
CEREAL	<.01	TANYA	<.01
CHUCK	<.01	TELEPHONE	<.01
COMMERCIAL	<.01	TIC-TAC-TOE	<.01
CONSTRICTOR	<.01	TIRE	<.01
CRAB	<.01	TRAP	<.01
CRAYONS	<.01	ABLE	<.01
CUTE	<.01	ANTS	<.01
DAIRY	<.01	BATS	<.01
DECIDED	<.01	BEING	<.01
EIGHTEEN	<.01	BOOTS	<.01
EVEL	<.01	BURIED	<.01
FLOAT	<.01	BUTCH	<.01
FRIENDLY	<.01	CARRY	<.01
GRAND	<.01	CATCHER	<.01
GRUFF	<.01	CHINNY	<.01
HAY	<.01	CLAY	<.01
HE'D	<.01	CLOSER	<.01
HELICOPTER	<.01	CLOWNS	<.01
HERSELF	<.01	COOKING	<.01
HISSELF*	<.01	COUNTRY	<.01
HOP	<.01	COUNTS	<.01
JIM	<.01	CUP	<.01
JOE	<.01	DINOSAURS	<.01
JOHNNY	<.01	DONKEY	<.01
KNIEVEL	<.01	DOODY	<.01
KNOCKS	<.01	EASTER	<.01
LATER	<.01	ELEPHANTS	<.01
LIBRARY	<.01	FINGERS	<.01
LOG	<.01	FINISHED	<.01
MATTER	<.01	FIXING	<.01
MICE	<.01	FLAGS	<.01
MINIBIKES	<.01	FLIP	<.01
NINETEEN	<.01	GOOD-BYE	<.01
PASTE	<.01	GUM	<.01
PENGUIN	<.01	HAYWORTH	<.01
POPCORN	<.01	HITTING	<.01
PORCH	<.01	HOPE	<.01
QUEEN	<.01	HORNS	<.01
READS	<.01	HOWDY	<.01
REDS	<.01	INCHES	<.01
RICH	<.01	INDIAN	<.01
ROLLS	<.01	JELLY	<.01
SAND	<.01	KAREN	<.01
SEA	<.01	KATHY	<.01

WORD	PERCENT	WORD	PERCENT
KNEE	<.01	BUSHES	<.01
LETTERS	<.01	CAPTAIN	<.01
MASK	<.01	CAST	<.01
MEAT	<.01	CHECKED	<.01
MESS	<.01	CHICAGO	<.01
MILL	<.01	CHRISTOPHER	<.01
MINE'S	<.01	CLIMBING	<.01
MISSY	<.01	COLLEGE	<.01
PAN	<.01	COLORING	<.01
PIGGIES	<.01	COUSIN'S	<.01
PONY	<.01	CRY	<.01
PRACTICE	<.01	DARTS	<.01
PUPPETS	<.01	DIG	<.01
PUSHING	<.01	DROPS	<.01
RABBITS	<.01	DROVE	<.01
RACING	<.01	ESPECIALLY	<.01
RAGGEDY	<.01	EXCITING	<.01
RECORDS	<.01	FARTHER	<.01
RIVER	<.01	FOLLOWED	<.01
RUSH	<.01	GILLIGAN	<.01
SANDWICHES	<.01	GLASSES	<.01
SHARK	<.01	GRAVEYARD	<.01
SITS	<.01	GUS	<.01
SMOKE	<.01	GUY'S	<.01
SPINS	<.01	HATES	<.01
STITCHES	<.01	HUFFED	<.01
TOE	<.01	HUNTING	<.01
TONGUE	<.01	HUT	<.01
TRACY	<.01	INVISIBLE	<.01
UGLY	<.01	JAY	<.01
WAKE	<.01	JOKES	<.01
WALT	<.01	JUNIOR	<.01
WEB	<.01	KENTUCKY	<.01
WHALE	<.01	KEY	<.01
WRECK	<.01	LAURIE	<.01
WRECKED	<.01	LESSONS	<.01
ACTS	<.01	LIFT	<.01
ALLOWED	<.01	LIZARD	<.01
APES	<.01	MEET	<.01
ASKING	<.01	MELTING	<.01
BATTER	<.01	MINIBIKE	<.01
BEES	<.01	MITT	<.01
BEGINNING	<.01	MOTOR	<.01
BESIDE	<.01	MOVES	<.01
BETTY	<.01	NEAR	<.01
BICYCLE	<.01	NEIGHBOR	<.01
BIGGEST	<.01	PARTRIDGE	<.01
BLOWS	<.01	PILLOW	<.01
BOO	<.01	PLATE	<.01
BUNK	<.01	PLUS	<.01

WORD	PERCENT	WORD	PERCENT
POND	<.01	CARROTS	<.01
POUR	<.01	CHAIN	<.01
PRESS	<.01	CHANCE	<.01
PUZZLE	<.01	CHANGE	<.01
RAIN	<.01	CLIMBS	<.01
RINGS	<.01	CORN	<.01
SANDWICH	<.01	COTTAGE	<.01
SCRATCHED	<.01	COUNTING	<.01
SENT	<.01	COVERS	<.01
SHERRY	<.01	CRIED	<.01
SIDEWALK	<.01	DAN	<.01
SKINNY	<.01	DAVID	<.01
SLOW	<.01	DEER	<.01
SMASHED	<.01	DOT	<.01
SNAKES	<.01	DOUGH	<.01
SONGS	<.01	DRAGON	<.01
SPORT	<.01	DRIVES	<.01
STACK	<.01	ELEPHANT	<.01
STEEL	<.01	ELEVATOR	<.01
SUN	<.01	EQUAL	<.01
SWEET	<.01	FELT	<.01
TEAR	<.01	FILLED	<.01
THANK	<.01	FILM	<.01
TORNADO	<.01	FONZ	<.01
TOUCHING	<.01	FREEZE	<.01
WALKS	<.01	FROSTY	<.01
WAX	<.01	FUNNIEST	<.01
WE'D	<.01	GANG	<.01
WHEELER	<.01	GIVING	<.01
WHOSE	<.01	GOB	<.01
WINGS	<.01	GREW	<.01
WORM	<.01	HAMMER	<.01
ADRIAN	<.01	HAPPEN	<.01
ANYONE	<.01	HILLS	<.01
ARMY	<.01	HOLDS	<.01
BEANSTALK	<.01	HOLLY	<.01
BELLY	<.01	KITTEN	<.01
BLUES	<.01	LAURA	<.01
BOWLS	<.01	LETTUCE	<.01
BOXING	<.01	LINDA	<.01
BOYFRIEND	<.01	MARIE	<.01
BREAKFAST	<.01	MARY	<.01
BRINGS	<.01	MOON	<.01
BUCKWHEAT	<.01	MUFFET	<.01
BUMP	<.01	ONTO	<.01
BUYS	<.01	OTHER'S	<.01
C	<.01	OVERNIGHT	<.01
CABIN	<.01	PADDLE	<.01
CANDYLAND	<.01	PARTS	<.01
CANES	<.01	PAYDAY	<.01

WORD	PERCENT	WORD	PERCENT
PICKS	<.01	BUTT	<.01
PLAYERS	<.01	CANS	<.01
PLAYGROUND	<.01	CAPTURED	<.01
PLUTO	<.01	CHANGED	<.01
PUFFED	<.01	CHASES	<.01
QUESTION	<.01	CHECK	<.01
RACES	<.01	CHUCKY	<.01
RECESS	<.01	COATS	<.01
RICKY	<.01	COVERED	<.01
RIDED*	<.01	DRACULA	<.01
ROSIE	<.01	DRAWING	<.01
ROY	<.01	ENGINE	<.01
S	<.01	EVERYBODY'S	<.01
SATURDAYS	<.01	FAIRY	<.01
SCARE	<.01	FALLED*	<.01
SEVENTEEN	<.01	FORTUNATELY	<.01
SHE'D	<.01	FOURTH	<.01
SHERIFF	<.01	GILLIGAN'S	<.01
SHOP	<.01	GRABBED	<.01
SIXTH	<.01	GRADERS	<.01
SKELETON	<.01	HANDLE	<.01
SKUNK	<.01	HANGED	<.01
SLAP	<.01	HAPPENS	<.01
SLID	<.01	HIGHEST	<.01
SMART	<.01	HIMSELF	<.01
SOAP	<.01	HUSBAND	<.01
SOCCER	<.01	INVITED	<.01
SOCKS	<.01	JIMMY	<.01
STEAL	<.01	KEN	<.01
STOLE	<.01	KITTY	<.01
STOPS	<.01	KNOCKING	<.01
STRIPED	<.01	LITTLER	<.01
STUPID	<.01	LITTLEST	<.01
THROWED*	<.01	MARCIA	<.01
TICKET	<.01	MICROPHONE	<.01
TIGHT	<.01	MIX	<.01
TRAPPED	<.01	MOTHERS	<.01
WALLY	<.01	NASTY	<.01
WOODEN	<.01	NET	<.01
WORMS	<.01	NICKY	<.01
WRITING	<.01	NOTE	<.01
YOURSELF	<.01	OPENS	<.01
ANT	<.01	OPERATION	<.01
AUNT'S	<.01	PENCILS	<.01
BARETTA	<.01	PIE	<.01
BATTLESHIP	<.01	PIN	<.01
BEATS	<.01	POISON	<.01
BEN	<.01	POTATOES	<.01
BERET	<.01	POUND	<.01
BOUNCES	<.01	POW	<.01

WORD	PERCENT	WORD	PERCENT
PUPPET	<.01	BURY	<.01
PUZZLES	<.01	BUSH	<.01
RACER	<.01	BYE	<.01
RANGER	<.01	CAROL	<.01
RANNED*	<.01	CARROT	<.01
ROGER	<.01	CEMENT	<.01
ROLLING	<.01	CHARLIE'S	<.01
ROUGH	<.01	CHERRIES	<.01
RUG	<.01	CIDER	<.01
SAD	<.01	CLOSEST	<.01
SEND	<.01	COFFEE	<.01
SINGS	<.01	COOKED	<.01
SINK	<.01	COTTON	<.01
SKATE	<.01	COYOTE	<.01
SPINNING	<.01	CRIES	<.01
STEPPED	<.01	CURSE	<.01
SWAM	<.01	DARREN	<.01
TOMATO	<.01	DART	<.01
TOWER	<.01	DIXIE	<.01
TRAPS	<.01	DRY	<.01
TREASURE	<.01	DUKES	<.01
TRIPPED	<.01	DYNAMITE	<.01
TROY	<.01	ELECTRIC	<.01
TURNING	<.01	ELSE'S	<.01
TWICE	<.01	ERIC	<.01
UNDERNEATH	<.01	EVE	<.01
WASHING	<.01	EVERYWHERE	<.01
WEE	<.01	FACES	<.01
WEISMILLER	<.01	FAKE	<.01
WHACK	<.01	FED	<.01
WHEREVER	<.01	FEELS	<.01
WHIPS	<.01	FISHES	<.01
WHISTLE	<.01	FIT	<.01
WILMA	<.01	FOLLOWING	<.01
YOU'D	<.01	FOUL	<.01
ABOMINABLE	<.01	FOXES	<.01
AMERICA	<.01	FRITZ	<.01
ANNA	<.01	GOLF	<.01
APARTMENTS	<.01	GRAMPA	<.01
ASKS	<.01	GRAVE	<.01
BAMM	<.01	GRAY	<.01
BIONICS	<.01	GROUP	<.01
BOBO	<.01	HATS	<.01
BOOGER	<.01	HAZZARD	<.01
BOXES	<.01	HEADACHE	<.01
BREAKING	<.01	HEARS	<.01
BREAKS	<.01	HIDING	<.01
BUILDED*	<.01	HO	<.01
BULB	<.01	IDEA	<.01
BUMPED	<.01	INDIANA	<.01

WORD	PERCENT	WORD	PERCENT
JACKET	<.01	STATE	<.01
JOB	<.01	STAYING	<.01
KANGAROO	<.01	STOVE	<.01
KISSING	<.01	SUCH	<.01
LACY	<.01	SWALLOWED	<.01
LADDERS	<.01	TALLER	<.01
LADIES	<.01	TANKS	<.01
LASSIE	<.01	TENT	<.01
LAYS	<.01	THINKING	<.01
LEARNING	<.01	TICKLES	<.01
LEAST	<.01	TIGERS	<.01
LOSER	<.01	TREK	<.01
LUCKY	<.01	TWINS	<.01
M	<.01	U	<.01
MELTED	<.01	UNDERDOG	<.01
MERRY	<.01	UNFORTUNATE	<.01
MESSED	<.01	UNICORN	<.01
MICHIGAN	<.01	WAITING	<.01
MOSTEST*	<.01	WALRUS	<.01
MUSEUM	<.01	ABC'S	<.01
NEEDED	<.01	ACCIDENT	<.01
NEITHER	<.01	ANGELA	<.01
OX	<.01	APACHE	<.01
PAD	<.01	ARROW	<.01
PARADE	<.01	ATTIC	<.01
PENCIL	<.01	BACON	<.01
PICNIC	<.01	BANG	<.01
PING-PONG	<.01	BARBIES	<.01
PLAIN	<.01	BASKETS	<.01
PLANT	<.01	BATTERIES	<.01
PRESLEY	<.01	BEER	<.01
PRETENDED	<.01	BEND	<.01
PRIZES	<.01	BETWEEN	<.01
PUPPIES	<.01	BLONDE	<.01
QUARTER	<.01	BOUNCED	<.01
RACCOON	<.01	BRAIN	<.01
RAINER	<.01	BRUSH	<.01
RAMPS	<.01	BUBBLE	<.01
RAY	<.01	BURNING	<.01
SAVE	<.01	BUSINESS	<.01
SERGEANT	<.01	CATCHED*	<.01
SHARE	<.01	CEILING	<.01
SHARING	<.01	CHEST	<.01
SHOULDERS	<.01	CHIEF	<.01
SIMON	<.01	CHIPMUNKS	<.01
SLEEPY	<.01	CHOOSE	<.01
SOMEPLACE	<.01	CLEANED	<.01
SPELL	<.01	COASTERS	<.01
SPLITS	<.01	COMMISSION	<.01
SPOON	<.01	COMPANY	<.01

WORD	PERCENT	WORD	PERCENT
COURT	<.01	LIGHTNING	<.01
CUPS	<.01	LINK	<.01
CYLONS	<.01	LIP	<.01
DADS	<.01	LOVED	<.01
DECK	<.01	MAIL	<.01
DENNIS	<.01	MATCHES	<.01
DICK	<.01	MATH	<.01
DING	<.01	MAY	<.01
DIVING	<.01	MICHAEL	<.01
DRAWED*	<.01	MIND	<.01
DRAWER	<.01	MONTHS	<.01
DREAM	<.01	MOTEL	<.01
DRUNK	<.01	MUMMY	<.01
EXPLODED	<.01	OURSELVES	<.01
FINISH	<.01	OUTS	<.01
FIRECRACKER	<.01	OWL	<.01
FLIPPER	<.01	PACK	<.01
FOLLOWS	<.01	PAGES	<.01
FRIGHTENED	<.01	PERSONS	<.01
FUNNEST*	<.01	PIPE	<.01
G	<.01	PLAYROOM	<.01
GALACTICA	<.01	POPS	<.01
GARDEN	<.01	PROPERTY	<.01
GATE	<.01	PUMPKINS	<.01
GEORGE	<.01	QUICK	<.01
GINGER	<.01	RAKE	<.01
GOD	<.01	RALPH	<.01
GORDON	<.01	RECORDING	<.01
GRANDPA'S	<.01	REMEMBERED	<.01
HEATHER	<.01	REPORTED	<.01
HECK	<.01	REVERSE	<.01
HINKLE	<.01	ROCKING	<.01
HOOP	<.01	RUBBER	<.01
HOPPED	<.01	SCORES	<.01
HULA	<.01	SHARKS	<.01
HURTING	<.01	SHELL	<.01
J	<.01	SHOPPING	<.01
JAMES	<.01	SHOWING	<.01
JAWS	<.01	SKIN	<.01
JEEP	<.01	SLIPPED	<.01
KARATE	<.01	SMELLED	<.01
KICKING	<.01	SON	<.01
KID'S	<.01	SOUTH	<.01
KIMBERLY	<.01	SPIDERS	<.01
KISS	<.01	SPLASH	<.01
KISSED	<.01	SPOTS	<.01
KRYPTONITE	<.01	STACY	<.01
L	<.01	STOLED*	<.01
LICKED	<.01	STUFFED	<.01
LIGAMENT	<.01	SUMMERS	<.01

WORD	PERCENT	WORD	PERCENT
SUNDAYS	<.01	CAP	<.01
SUPPOSE	<.01	CAPE	<.01
T	<.01	CAPTURE	<.01
TANK	<.01	CAREFUL	<.01
TAUGHT	<.01	CARTWHEELS	<.01
TEACH	<.01	CAVES	<.01
TEACHER'S	<.01	CENTER	<.01
TENNESSEE	<.01	CHARLIES	<.01
THEIRS	<.01	CHINA	<.01
THURSDAY	<.01	CHOO	<.01
TINY	<.01	CHRISSY	<.01
TOMMY	<.01	CHUTES	<.01
TOPS	<.01	CLEANING	<.01
TREATING	<.01	CLIFF	<.01
TUMMY	<.01	CLOUDS	<.01
TWIRL	<.01	COACH	<.01
ULTRA	<.01	COKE	<.01
UNO	<.01	COLORADO	<.01
WAITED	<.01	CONES	<.01
WAR	<.01	COP	<.01
WEDDING	<.01	COSTUMES	<.01
WELCOME	<.01	COUNTY	<.01
WHEELIE	<.01	COURSE	<.01
WICKED	<.01	COVER	<.01
WINNING	<.01	CRACKED	<.01
WIRE	<.01	CRIME	<.01
WITCHES	<.01	CROOKS	<.01
WORE	<.01	CUTTING	<.01
Y'ALL	<.01	D	<.01
YELLING	<.01	DAISY	<.01
AARDVARK	<.01	DALLAS	<.01
ACCIDENTAL	<.01	DARN	<.01
ALICE	<.01	DEBBIE'S	<.01
ALLIGATORS	<.01	DEVIL	<.01
ANKLE	<.01	DIAL	<.01
ASHES	<.01	DINO	<.01
BABYSITTER	<.01	DISAPPEARED	<.01
BALLOONS	<.01	DIVE	<.01
BARKING	<.01	DOGHOUSE	<.01
BATTLESTAR	<.01	DON	<.01
BELLS	<.01	DOUG	<.01
BLOWING	<.01	DRESSES	<.01
BORING	<.01	DRINKING	<.01
BOUNCING	<.01	DRINKS	<.01
BRANCHES	<.01	DRIPPING	<.01
BRANG*	<.01	EAR	<.01
BROWNIE	<.01	EATEN	<.01
BUST	<.01	ERASE	<.01
BUZZ	<.01	ERASER	<.01
CAKES	<.01	ESCAPE	<.01

WORD	PERCENT	WORD	PERCENT
EXCUSE	<.01	PHILLIP	<.01
F	<.01	PITCH	<.01
FLIPPED	<.01	PLUG	<.01
FLOATING	<.01	POLICEMEN	<.01
FONZIE	<.01	PRACTICING	<.01
FOUGHT	<.01	PRINCESS	<.01
FREEZING	<.01	PUP	<.01
FRUIT	<.01	QUESTIONS	<.01
GLOVE	<.01	QUITE	<.01
GLUE	<.01	RAISE	<.01
GROCERIES	<.01	RATTLESNAKE	<.01
GROWING	<.01	REACH	<.01
HOG	<.01	REFRIGERATOR	<.01
HOLLERED	<.01	REGULAR	<.01
HUG	<.01	RHINO	<.01
HUGE	<.01	ROB	<.01
HUNDREDS	<.01	ROBBER	<.01
INDIANAPOLIS	<.01	ROCKETS	<.01
JAR	<.01	RUMPLESTILTSKIN	<.01
JESUS	<.01	SAVES	<.01
JUICE	<.01	SCARF	<.01
JUNE	<.01	SEVENTY	<.01
KATE	<.01	SHADOW	<.01
KILLS	<.01	SHIMMY	<.01
KNEES	<.01	SHIRTS	<.01
LAMP	<.01	SHOTGUN	<.01
LANDING	<.01	SIDES	<.01
LEAGUE	<.01	SIMPLE	<.01
LEE	<.01	SKATES	<.01
LID	<.01	SLED	<.01
LOGAN'S	<.01	SLIDES	<.01
LORI	<.01	SOCKO	<.01
LOW	<.01	SOUNDS	<.01
MACARONI	<.01	SPANKING	<.01
MARTY	<.01	SPLASHED	<.01
MIDNIGHT	<.01	SPRAYED	<.01
MODELS	<.01	STAPLED	<.01
NIGHTS	<.01	STARS	<.01
NINETY	<.01	STRATEGO	<.01
NONSENSE	<.01	SUITS	<.01
NOVEMBER	<.01	SWAT	<.01
NURSE	<.01	SWIMMED*	<.01
NUTS	<.01	SWINGING	<.01
OFTEN	<.01	TACKLED	<.01
OURS	<.01	TASTING	<.01
PAIL	<.01	TEA	<.01
PARTNER	<.01	TEARS	<.01
PASSED	<.01	TERRY	<.01
PEGS	<.01	THEY'VE	<.01
PEOPLE'S	<.01	TIGGER	<.01

WORD	PERCENT	WORD	PERCENT
TIMMY	<.01	BRAD	<.01
TOM-TOM	<.01	BRAKE	<.01
TRADE	<.01	BRAKES	<.01
TUFFET	<.01	BROKED*	<.01
TUNNEL	<.01	BRUISE	<.01
TURTLES	<.01	BRUNG*	<.01
TWEET	<.01	BUBBLES	<.01
TWIST	<.01	BULLS	<.01
TWOS	<.01	BUMPS	<.01
UNCOMFORTABLE	<.01	BUMPY	<.01
USES	<.01	BUTCHER	<.01
USING	<.01	BUYER	<.01
VILLAGE	<.01	CABBAGE	<.01
VOLLEYBALL	<.01	CABINET	<.01
WASHED	<.01	CAGES	<.01
WEEKEND	<.01	CALIFORNIA	<.01
WENDY	<.01	CARRYING	<.01
WHALES	<.01	CAT'S	<.01
WHAM	<.01	CELLAR	<.01
WHIP	<.01	CHALK	<.01
WHIPPING	<.01	CHALKBOARD	<.01
WIDE	<.01	CHARACTER	<.01
WIPED	<.01	CHECKER	<.01
WRAPPED	<.01	CHEF	<.01
WRESTLING	<.01	CHER	<.01
YAHTZEE	<.01	CHERRY	<.01
ACROBATS	<.01	CHESS	<.01
ALFALFA'S	<.01	CHICKS	<.01
ALLEY	<.01	CHILDREN'S	<.01
ALLISON	<.01	CLOSING	<.01
ANDREA	<.01	COLLIE	<.01
ANNETTE	<.01	CONTROL	<.01
ANSWER	<.01	COUNTED	<.01
ANYWHERE	<.01	CURTAIN	<.01
ART	<.01	DANCE	<.01
AVENUE	<.01	DANCED	<.01
AWAKE	<.01	DANCING	<.01
AWFUL	<.01	DANNY	<.01
BAKE	<.01	DEANA	<.01
BANANAS	<.01	DEBBIE	<.01
BATHTUB	<.01	DIANE	<.01
BEAVER	<.01	DICES*	<.01
BEDROOMS	<.01	DISNEYLAND	<.01
BELTS	<.01	DOLLY	<.01
BILLS	<.01	DOMINOES	<.01
BING	<.01	DONUTS	<.01
BITES	<.01	DOTS	<.01
BOARDS	<.01	DRANK	<.01
BOBBER	<.01	DREAMING	<.01
BOING	<.01	DRIVER	<.01

WORD	PERCENT	WORD	PERCENT
EAGLE	<.01	MIKEY	<.01
EXPLAIN	<.01	MILES	<.01
EXPLODE	<.01	MINES	<.01
FESTIVAL	<.01	MONDAY	<.01
FIGHTED*	<.01	MONTH	<.01
FIREHOUSE	<.01	MORNINGS	<.01
FIREMAN	<.01	MS.	<.01
FLIPS	<.01	N	<.01
FOLDED	<.01	NAUGHTY	<.01
FOOL .	<.01	NINES	<.01
FRANKENSTEIN	<.01	NOISES	<.01
FRANKIE	<.01	NORTH	<.01
FRECKLES	<.01	NOSED	<.01
GALEN	<.01	OLDEST	<.01
GARBAGE	<.01	OPENING	<.01
GIANTS	<.01	ORANGES	<.01
GORGO	<.01	OSCAR	<.01
GORILLAS	<.01	OURSELF*	<.01
GRAB	<.01	OUTFIELD	<.01
GROWN	<.01	OUTFIT	<.01
GUEST	<.01	OWNER	<.01
GYMNASTICS	<.01	PADS	<.01
HAIRY	<.01	PAINTS	<.01
HARDEST	<.01	PAIRS	<.01
HELMETS	<.01	PAJAMAS	<.01
HOLDED*	<.01	PANCAKES	<.01
HOPSCOTCH	<.01	PARACHUTE	<.01
HOURS	<.01	PATH	<.01
ILLINOIS	<.01	PAWS	<.01
INNING	<.01	PEDAL	<.01
JACKIE	<.01	PEGGY	<.01
JANE	<.01	PEPPER	<.01
JODI	<.01	PHILIPPINE	<.01
JOKE	<.01	PIG'S	<.01
JONES	<.01	PIGLET	<.01
K	<.01	PILLOWS	<.01
KILEY	<.01	PINCH	<.01
LAP	<.01	PIXIE	<.01
LETTING	<.01	PLANES	<.01
LISTENED	<.01	POCKETS	<.01
LONE	<.01	PONIES	<.01
LOOP	<.01	PUMP	<.01
LOWER	<.01	PURSE	<.01
LYING	<.01	PUSHES	<.01
MANGER	<.01	RAILROAD	<.01
MARCY	<.01	RAINBOW	<.01
MASKS	<.01	RASH	<.01
MASTER	<.01	RED-TAIL	<.01
MEDICINE	<.01	ROCKED	<.01
MIDNIGHTS	<.01	ROGERS	<.01

WORD	PERCENT	WORD	PERCENT
ROSES	<.01	TALE	<.01
RULES	<.01	TAMMY	<.01
RUNWAY	<.01	TASTES	<.01
SACK	<.01	TEAMS	<.01
SAMMY	<.01	TEARING	<.01
SANDY	<.01	TEST	<.01
SANG	<.01	THAT-A-WAY	<.01
SARAH	<.01	THEMSELVES	<.01
SAUCE	<.01	THIRSTY	<.01
SCARECROW	<.01	THROAT	<.01
SCIENCE	<.01	TIN	<.01
SCOTTS	<.01	TINA	<.01
SCREAMS	<.01	TIRES	<.01
SEATS	<.01	TODD	<.01
SELL	<.01	TOUCHED	<.01
SHAPED	<.01	TRACKS	<.01
SHARON	<.01	TRAIL	<.01
SHEEP	<.01	TRAILERS	<.01
SHEET	<.01	TRICKED	<.01
SHINY	<.01	TROOP	<.01
SIGNED	<.01	TUMBLING	<.01
SINGLE	<.01	TWENTY-FIVE	<.01
SKIING	<.01	TWISTED	<.01
SKIPPER	<.01	TWISTER	<.01
SLAPPED	<.01	TYLER	<.01
SNEAK	<.01	UNFROZEN	<.01
SOLDIER	<.01	VANILLA	<.01
SORE	<.01	VISITING	<.01
SPANK	<.01	VOICES	<.01
SPENT	<.01	VOTE	<.01
SPILL	<.01	WAKING	<.01
SPILLED	<.01	WALLPAPER	<.01
SPOOK	<.01	WASHINGTON	<.01
SPRAY	<.01	WAVE	<.01
SPRING	<.01	WAVES	<.01
SPUD	<.01	WEARS	<.01
STAGE	<.01	WEEDS	<.01
STANDS	<.01	WEIRD	<.01
STARING	<.01	WHIPPED	<.01
STEALS	<.01	WISHING	<.01
STEERING	<.01	WOODSTOCK	<.01
STEW	<.01	WORKED	<.01
STICKED*	<.01	YAKS	<.01
STORES	<.01	YELLED	<.01
STRIKE	<.01	ABOVE	<.01
STRONGER	<.01	ACTED	<.01
SURPRISES	<.01	ACTING	<.01
SURROUNDED	<.01	ADD	<.01
TAILS	<.01	AGGRAVATION	<.01
TAKED*	<.01	APPLE'S	<.01

WORD	PERCENT	WORD	PERCENT
APRIL	<.01	CENTS	<.01
ARCHIES	<.01	CHECKS	<.01
ARKANSAS	<.01	CHEERIO	<.01
ARNOLD'S	<.01	CHILD	<.01
ARROWS	<.01	CHIPS	<.01
AUSTIN'S	<.01	CHOSE	<.01
BAA	<.01	CINCINNATI	<.01
BAKED	<.01	CLASSROOM	<.01
BALLOON	<.01	COMB	<.01
BANDAGE	<.01	COMICS	<.01
BANDAIDS	<.01	CONSTRUCTION	<.01
BARBECUE	<.01	COPS	<.01
BARBIE	<.01	CORRAL	<.01
BARNACLE	<.01	CRACKERS	<.01
BARRETTE	<.01	CRAWLED	<.01
BATH	<.01	CRAYON	<.01
BATTLING	<.01	CREATURES	<.01
BEA	<.01	CREEPS	<.01
BEAN	<.01	CREEPY	<.01
BEAUTIFUL	<.01	CRICKET	<.01
BECKY	<.01	CROSSING	<.01
BENDED*	<.01	CROWN	<.01
BITTY	<.01	CRUNCHING	<.01
BLACKTOP	<.01	CRUTCHES	<.01
BLANKET	<.01	CURDS	<.01
BLENDER	<.01	CURLS	<.01
BLUTO	<.01	CURLY	<.01
BO	<.01	CYCLE	<.01
BOBBIN	<.01	CYLON	<.01
BOLOGNA	<.01	DAB	<.01
BOZO'S	<.01	DADA	<.01
BREAKER	<.01	DADDY-O	<.01
BRIAR	<.01	DAM	<.01
BRINGED*	<.01	DANGER	<.01
BUDDY	<.01	DANGEROUS	<.01
BULLDOG	<.01	DARREN'S	<.01
BULLET	<.01	DAWN	<.01
BULLETS	<.01	DAYTIME	<.01
BUNS	<.01	DEE	<.01
BURGER	<.01	DENTIST	<.01
CANNON	<.01	DERBY	<.01
CANYON	<.01	DEWEY	<.01
CARES	<.01	DIAPER	<.01
CARPETING	<.01	DIAPERS	<.01
CARRIES	<.01	DISNEYWORLD	<.01
CARTWHEEL	<.01	DOCK	<.01
CAT'S-EYE	<.01	DONG	<.01
CATCHERS	<.01	DONKEYS	<.01
CATFISH	<.01	DOPE	<.01
CATHY	<.01	DRAG	<.01

WORD	PERCENT	WORD	PERCENT
DRAINED	<.01	HONEYMOON	<.01
DRESSERS	<.01	HOPPING	<.01
DRESSING	<.01	HORSEBACK	<.01
DRIED	<.01	HOSE	<.01
DRIVEWAY	<.01	HOTEL	<.01
DUKE	<.01	HOWARD	<.01
DUMP	<.01	HUM	<.01
DURING	<.01	HUMAN	<.01
E	<.01	HUNTER	<.01
ELECTRICITY	<.01	HUP	<.01
ENDING	<.01	ICING	<.01
ERNIE	<.01	INCH	<.01
FACTORY	<.01	INTRODUCING	<.01
FASTEST	<.01	JACKY	<.01
FIGURE	<.01	JANET	<.01
FINDING	<.01	JED	<.01
FIREPLACE	<.01	JENNIFER	<.01
FLASH	<.01	JENNY	<.01
FRISBEE	<.01	JESSIE	<.01
FROGS	<.01	JOHN'S	<.01
FROZE	<.01	KAY	<.01
FUR	<.01	KEEPED*	<.01
FURNITURE	<.01	KEEPER	<.01
GAR	<.01	KEITH	<.01
GARRETT	<.01	KETCHUP	<.01
GERMAN	<.01	KIDDIE	<.01
GIRAFFES	<.01	KISSES	<.01
GLOVES	<.01	LADY'S	<.01
GOLDAR	<.01	LAMPS	<.01
GOODIES	<.01	LAUNDROMAT	<.01
GOOFY	<.01	LAVERNE	<.01
GRANDFATHER	<.01	LEADER	<.01
GRAS	<.01	LEAN	<.01
GRINCH	<.01	LEASH	<.01
GRIZZLY	<.01	LICKS	<.01
GROCERY	<.01	LIFTED	<.01
GUITAR	<.01	LILY	<.01
H	<.01	LISA'S	<.01
HALL	<.01	LISTENING	<.01
HAMMERS	<.01	LIT	<.01
HAMSTERS	<.01	LOADED	<.01
HART	<.01	LOCK	<.01
HATED	<.01	LOCKER	<.01
HAWAII	<.01	LOVING	<.01
HELMET	<.01	LUCY	<.01
HEN	<.01	LUKE	<.01
HIGHLAND	<.01	MAGOO	<.01
HIKING	<.01	MARDI	<.01
HIPPOPOTAMUS	<.01	MASH	<.01
HOBBY	<.01	MATIC	<.01

WORD	PERCENT	WORD	PERCENT
MATTRESS	<.01	QUEER	<.01
MEDIUM	<.01	QUIZ	<.01
MENACE	<.01	R	<.01
MENS*	<.01	RAG	<.01
MEOW	<.01	RANDY	<.01
MICHELLE	<.01	RANG	<.01
MINNIE	<.01	REINDEER	<.01
MIXED	<.01	RESTAURANT	<.01
MO	<.01	RICHIE	<.01
MOBY	<.01	RIPPED	<.01
MONORAIL	<.01	ROBBED	<.01
MOTELS	<.01	ROD	<.01
MUSHROOMS	<.01	ROO	<.01
NAP	<.01	ROSCOE	<.01
NEEDS	<.01	ROSIES	<.01
NEIGHBOR'S	<.01	RUFF	<.01
NETS	<.01	RUSH'S	<.01
NINTH	<.01	SAILOR	<.01
NOON	<.01	SANTY	<.01
NOTES	<.01	SAVING	<.01
OCTOPUS	<.01	SCARES	<.01
OPIE	<.01	SCARING	<.01
OUTDOORS	<.01	SCOOT	<.01
PACKS	<.01	SCOOTER	<.01
PAL	<.01	SCRAPE	<.01
PARROT	<.01	SCREAM	<.01
PARTNERS	<.01	SEAL	<.01
PASSING	<.01	SEALS	<.01
PAUL'S	<.01	SEAN	<.01
PEANUTS	<.01	SEED	<.01
PEBBLES	<.01	SEEMS	<.01
PENNSYLVANIA	<.01	SELLING	<.01
PEOPLES	<.01	SEWED	<.01
PIGEON	<.01	SHANNA	<.01
PILED	<.01	SHAPE	<.01
PLAN	<.01	SHAWNEE	<.01
PLATES	<.01	SHELF	<.01
POLAR	<.01	SHELLS	<.01
POLLY	<.01	SHEPHERD	<.01
POPSICLES	<.01	SHORE	<.01
PORCHES	<.01	SHOWER	<.01
POST	<.01	SHUMAN	<.01
POTSIE	<.01	SIDEWAYS	<.01
POWER	<.01	SINKING	<.01
PROMISED	<.01	SITTER	<.01
PUDDING	<.01	SIXTY	<.01
PUDDLE	<.01	SKIDDING	<.01
PULLS	<.01	SKIP	<.01
PUTTED*	<.01	SLICK	<.01
QUACK	<.01	SLIP	<.01

WORD	PERCENT	WORD	PERCENT
SNEAKS	<.01	THIN	<.01
SNOOPY'S	<.01	TICKETS	<.01
SNOWBALL	<.01	TIM	<.01
SNOWED	<.01	TOAST	<.01
SNOWY	<.01	TOILET	<.01
SOLD	<.01	TOOKEN*	<.01
SPANKED	<.01	TOSS	<.01
SPANNER	<.01	TOTO	<.01
SPEAK	<.01	TOUCHDOWNS	<.01
SPELLING	<.01	TOUCHES	<.01
SPEND	<.01	TOUGH	<.01
SPINNED*	<.01	TREATS	<.01
SPIT	<.01	TRIPS	<.01
SPOONS	<.01	TROPPING	<.01
SPRINGS	<.01	TUESDAY	<.01
SQUIRRELS	<.01	UNCLE'S	<.01
SQUIRT	<.01	UNDERGROUND	<.01
STATES	<.01	UNDERWATER	<.01
STATUE	<.01	UNFROZE	<.01
STEAK	<.01	UNIFORM	<.01
STEALED*	<.01	UNTIED	<.01
STEALING	<.01	VEGETABLES	<.01
STICKERS	<.01	WALLS	<.01
STING	<.01	WANTING	<.01
STOOL	<.01	WATERMELON	<.01
STOPPING	<.01	WAVING	<.01
STORM	<.01	WHEAT	<.01
STREETS	<.01	WIPE	<.01
STRIKES	<.01	WISHES	<.01
STRIPES	<.01	WOLFS*	<.01
STRONS	<.01	WORRY	<.01
SUBMARINE	<.01	YELL	<.01
SUCKED	<.01	ACTION	<.01
SUDDEN	<.01	ADAM	<.01
SUGAR	<.01	AFRICA	<.01
SUNK	<.01	ALL'S	<.01
SWATTER	<.01	AMY	<.01
SWORD	<.01	ANGEL	<.01
TARGET	<.01	ANGRY	<.01
TAXES	<.01	ANSWERS	<.01
TAYLOR	<.01	ANTIQUE	<.01
TEASE	<.01	AQUAMAN	<.01
TEDDY	<.01	ARCHIE	<.01
TEENSY	<.01	ARRESTED	<.01
TEENY	<.01	ARTIST	<.01
TELLED*	<.01	ATTACK	<.01
TENDER	<.01	ATTACKS	<.01
TERRIBLE	<.01	AUDIENCE	<.01
THANKS	<.01	BADDEST*	<.01
THEY'S*	<.01	BADGE	<.01

WORD	PERCENT	WORD	PERCENT
BAGS	<.01	BUNNIES	<.01
BAIT	<.01	BURNETT	<.01
BALANCE	<.01	BUSES	<.01
BANDAGED	<.01	BUSY	<.01
BANKS	<.01	BUTTONED	<.01
BAPTIZED	<.01	CAMED	<.01
BARELY	<.01	CAMERA	<.01
BARK	<.01	CAMPS	<.01
BARKS	<.01	CANDIES	<.01
BARRETTES	<.01	CANOE	<.01
BATGIRL	<.01	CAPITAL	<.01
BATHING	<.01	CAPTAINS	<.01
BATMOBILE	<.01	CARDBOARD	<.01
BATTING	<.01	CASTED*	<.01
BATTLE	<.01	CASTLES	<.01
BAY	<.01	CATSUP	<.01
BB	<.01	CELEBRATE	<.01
BEATED*	<.01	CEMETERY	<.01
BEATING	<.01	CERTAIN	<.01
BEETLES	<.01	CHARACTERS	<.01
BEGGING	<.01	CHARLES	<.01
BEHAVE	<.01	CHARLOTTE	<.01
BELONGED	<.01	CHEAT	<.01
BELOW	<.01	CHEWING	<.01
BENT	<.01	CHICK	<.01
BEWITCHED	<.01	CHIP	<.01
BIB	<.01	CHOPPER	<.01
BLADE	<.01	CHRIS'S	<.01
BLEEDING	<.01	CHRYSLER	<.01
BLOODY	<.01	CHUTE	<.01
BOATING	<.01	CIGAR	<.01
BOBO'S	<.01	CLAP	<.01
BOILING	<.01	CLARK	<.01
BONANZA	<.01	CLOUD	<.01
BOONE	<.01	COBRA	<.01
BORROW	<.01	COCOA	<.01
BOTTLES	<.01	COLDER	<.01
BOW	<.01	COLLAR	<.01
BOXED	<.01	COLLECT	<.01
BRANCH	<.01	COLLECTION	<.01
BRANT	<.01	COLUMINY	<.01
BRIDE	<.01	COMMANDER	<.01
BRIDGES	<.01	CONCRETE	<.01
BRIGHT	<.01	COOKS	<.01
BRUISED	<.01	COOTIE	<.01
BUBBS	<.01	COPY	<.01
BUFFALO	<.01	CORKY	<.01
BUG	<.01	COST	<.01
BULL'S-EYES	<.01	COSTUME	<.01
BUMPER	<.01	COUGAR	<.01

WORD	PERCENT	WORD	PERCENT
COW'S	<.01	EILEEN	<.01
CRABS	<.01	ELLER	<.01
CRACK	<.01	ENDED	<.01
CRACKING	<.01	ENEMY	<.01
CRAWLING	<.01	EVERYDAY	<.01
CREEK	<.01	EXACTLY	<.01
CRIB	<.01	EXIT	<.01
CROOKED	<.01	FAN	<.01
CRYSTAL	<.01	FEBRUARY	<.01
CUMBERLAND	<.01	FEEDED*	<.01
CUNNINGHAM	<.01	FEEDING	<.01
CYCLES	<.01	FIELDERS	<.01
DAN'S	<.01	FIGHTERS	<.01
DANCES	<.01	FILL	<.01
DANIEL	<.01	FILMS	<.01
DARNELL	<.01	FINE	<.01
DAUGHTER	<.01	FISHED	<.01
DEEPER	<.01	FISHERMAN	<.01
DEMON	<.01	FISHY	<.01
DETECTIVES	<.01	FITS	<.01
DIAMOND	<.01	FLATTEN	<.01
DIES	<.01	FLIED	<.01
DIGGED*	<.01	FLOATED	<.01
DIGGING	<.01	FLUFFY	<.01
DIME	<.01	FOLKS	<.01
DISH	<.01	FOOTSTEPS	<.01
DOC	<.01	FORCE	<.01
DOLPHIN	<.01	FORK	<.01
DOLPHINS	<.01	FORMULA	<.01
DONUT	<.01	FORWARD	<.01
DOWNS	<.01	FOZZI	<.01
DREAMED	<.01	FRAME	<.01
DRESSER	<.01	FRASER	<.01
DRIP	<.01	FREDDY	<.01
DROPPING	<.01	FRENCH	<.01
DROWN	<.01	FRIED	<.01
DROWNING	<.01	FROSTING	<.01
DRUMS	<.01	FRUITS	<.01
DUG	<.01	FRYING	<.01
DUMBO	<.01	FUDD	<.01
DUNGEON	<.01	FUDGE	<.01
DUO	<.01	FUNNIES	<.01
DWAYNE	<.01	GAIL	<.01
DYKE	<.01	GENERAL	<.01
DYNAMIC	<.01	GENTLEMEN	<.01
EARN	<.01	GEORGIE	<.01
EDDIE'S	<.01	GIFT	<.01
EDGE	<.01	GIRAFFE	<.01
EDITH	<.01	GLENN	<.01
EIFFEL	<.01	GOALS	<.01

WORD	PERCENT	WORD	PERCENT
GODMOTHER	<.01	JOINED	<.01
GOLDEN	<.01	JUDY	<.01
GOLDFISH	<.01	JULIE	<.01
GONG	<.01	KEARNEY	<.01
GOO	<.01	KIDDING	<.01
GOODIE	<.01	KIDNAPPED	<.01
GRABBING	<.01	KIKI	<.01
GREATEST	<.01	KILLER	<.01
GRIFFITH	<.01	KILLING	<.01
GRINDING	<.01	KITTENS	<.01
GROUCH	<.01	LAD	<.01
GROVER	<.01	LAFAYETTE	<.01
GROWED*	<.01	LARGE	<.01
GROWS	<.01	LARRY	<.01
GUESTS	<.01	LATELY	<.01
HALLWAY	<.01	LAUGHS	<.01
HAM	<.01	LAUNDRY	<.01
HAMBURGER	<.01	LAWN	<.01
HANDED	<.01	LEAD	<.01
HANDKERCHIEF	<.01	LEADS	<.01
HANDLEBARS	<.01	LEAF	<.01
HASN'T	<.01	LEANING	<.01
HAWK	<.01	LEAVED*	<.01
HEADLESS	<.01	LEAVING	<.01
HEAVEN	<.01	LEDGE	<.01
HEROES	<.01	LEGOS	<.01
HIKES	<.01	LEMON	<.01
HIM'S*	<.01	LEVER	<.01
HOGAN'S	<.01	LIFTS	<.01
HOLIDAY	<.01	LIGHTED*	<.01
HOMESTEAD	<.01	LINCOLN	<.01
HOPS	<.01	LONGER	<.01
HORN	<.01	LOOPS	<.01
HORSEMAN	<.01	LOUISE	<.01
HOWEVER	<.01	MACH	<.01
HUMANS	<.01	MACHINES	<.01
HUNT	<.01	MAGAZINE	<.01
HURRIED	<.01	MAGNIFYING	<.01
ICKY	<.01	MAID	<.01
IDENTITY	<.01	MAKERS	<.01
ILL	<.01	MAKEUP	<.01
INSURANCE	<.01	MALL	<.01
INTEREST	<.01	MANSION	<.01
IRONMAN	<.01	MARCH	<.01
JACK-O-LANTERN	<.01	MARCO	<.01
JACKETS	<.01	MARKET	<.01
JANUARY	<.01	MARKLAND	<.01
JEANS	<.01	MARKS	<.01
JET	<.01	MASHED	<.01
JEWISH	<.01	MATT	<.01

WORD	PERCENT	WORD	PERCENT
MAX	<.01	PETE	<.01
MEADOW	<.01	PIANO	<.01
MERRY-GO-ROUND	<.01	PIES	<.01
MESSES	<.01	PING	<.01
MIAMI	<.01	PINKY	<.01
MIGHTY	<.01	PINNED	<.01
MILE	<.01	PISTOLS	<.01
MILLER	<.01	PITCHES	<.01
MILLIONS	<.01	PITCHING	<.01
MINNESOTA	<.01	PLANTS	<.01
MINNOWS	<.01	PLUSES	<.01
MISSES	<.01	POCKETKNIFE	<.01
MISSING	<.01	POEM	<.01
MITTENS	<.01	POLO	<.01
MODEL	<.01	POODLE	<.01
MOMS	<.01	POSIES	<.01
MONSTER'S	<.01	POUNDING	<.01
MOOD	<.01	PRACTICALLY	<.01
MYSTERY	<.01	PREGNANT	<.01
NAIL	<.01	PRETENDS	<.01
NANCY	<.01	PRINCE	<.01
NATHAN	<.01	PRISON	<.01
NEAREST	<.01	PROGRAMS	<.01
NECKLACE	<.01	PROTECT	<.01
NECKS	<.01	PUCK	<.01
NEIGHBORHOOD	<.01	PUNISHED	<.01
NEIGHBORS	<.01	PURDUE	<.01
NEWSPAPER	<.01	QUARTERBACK	<.01
NOISY	<.01	RACCOONS	<.01
NURSERY	<.01	RACOON	<.01
NURSING	<.01	RAINED	<.01
NUT	<.01	RANGERS	<.01
OCTOBER	<.01	RAT	<.01
OUGHT	<.01	RAYS	<.01
OUTFIELDER	<.01	READER	<.01
OWNED	<.01	REASON	<.01
PAIR	<.01	RECEIVER	<.01
PALACE	<.01	RECESSES	<.01
PAMMY	<.01	REINDEERS*	<.01
PARADES	<.01	RESCUE	<.01
PARENTS	<.01	RESERVOIR	<.01
PARROTS	<.01	REVIEW	<.01
PARTIES	<.01	RHYMES	<.01
PARTLY	<.01	RICARDO	<.01
PATCHES	<.01	RICK	<.01
PEA	<.01	RIFLE	<.01
PEAS	<.01	RIFLEMAN	<.01
PEEKED	<.01	ROBBING	<.01
PEN	<.01	ROBERT	<.01
PENS	<.01	ROOMS	<.01

WORD	PERCENT	WORD	PERCENT
ROPES	<.01	SMOKES	<.01
ROTTEN	<.01	SNEAKED	<.01
ROVER	<.01	SNEAKING	<.01
RUB	<.01	SNEEZE	<.01
RUBBED	<.01	SNIFFS	<.01
RUINED	<.01	SNOWBALLS	<.01
SALAD	<.01	SOCIAL	<.01
SANTA'S	<.01	SOCK	<.01
SCHAFER	<.01	SODAS	<.01
SCOTTY	<.01	SOFTBALL	<.01
SCOTTY'S	<.01	SOLDIERS	<.01
SCREAMED	<.01	SOMERSAULT	<.01
SCREW	<.01	SPACESHIPS	<.01
SEEKER	<.01	SPACY	<.01
SELF	<.01	SPILLING	<.01
SENDS	<.01	SPOILED	<.01
SENSE	<.01	SQUAD	<.01
SHAN'T	<.01	SQUEAK	<.01
SHANNON	<.01	SQUEEZE	<.01
SHAPES	<.01	SQUIRTS	<.01
SHAWN	<.01	STABBED	<.01
SHEILA	<.01	STEER	<.01
SHINES	<.01	STEPPING	<.01
SHIRLEY	<.01	STEVEN	<.01
SHOCKED	<.01	STICKY	<.01
SHOOTED*	<.01	STINKED*	<.01
SHOULDN'T	<.01	STOCKING	<.01
SHOVED	<.01	STONES	<.01
SIGHT	<.01	STOOD	<.01
SIGNS	<.01	STRAWS	<.01
SILLIEST	<.01	STRIPE	<.01
SIR	<.01	STRUCK	<.01
SIREN	<.01	STUDIED	<.01
SITTEN*	<.01	STUDIES	<.01
SITTERS	<.01	STUNK	<.01
SIZZLERS	<.01	SUB	<.01
SKELETONS	<.01	SUCKER	<.01
SKIES	<.01	SUCKERS	<.01
SKINNED	<.01	SUDDENLY	<.01
SKIPS	<.01	SUE	<.01
SLAM	<.01	SUPERFRIENDS	<.01
SLAW	<.01	SWEEP	<.01
SLEIGH	<.01	SWIMS	<.01
SLIDING	<.01	SWISS	<.01
SMACKED	<.01	SWITCH	<.01
SMALLER	<.01	SWORDFISH	<.01
SMASH	<.01	SYCAMORE	<.01
SMEAR	<.01	TACKLES	<.01
SMEARED	<.01	TAKEN	<.01
SMELLS	<.01	TAMED	<.01

WORD	PERCENT	WORD	PERCENT
TAN	<.01	WEDNESDAY	<.01
TAPPED	<.01	WEIGHT	<.01
TAPPING	<.01	WEREWOLF	<.01
TAPS	<.01	WESTERN	<.01
TARGETS	<.01	WHACKED	<.01
TARZAN	<.01	WHEELIES	<.01
TASK	<.01	WHEY	<.01
TEACHERS	<.01	WHISKEY	<.01
TED	<.01	WHISTLED	<.01
TEE	<.01	WHOEVER'S	<.01
TEETER	<.01	WIGGLEY	<.01
TERESA	<.01	WILLIAM	<.01
TESTING	<.01	WINNERS	<.01
THELMA	<.01	WOO	<.01
THEMS*	<.01	WRENCH	<.01
THIMBLE	<.01	YELLS	<.01
THING'S	<.01	ZEBRA	<.01
THOMPSON	<.01	ZIMBA	<.01
THORN	<.01	ZIP	<.01
THOUSANDS	<.01	ABOARD	<.01
THUNDERBOLT	<.01	ABRAHAM	<.01
TIFFANY	<.01	ACHE	<.01
TIGHTROPE	<.01	ACORNS	<.01
TINKERBELL	<.01	ACRES	<.01
TOES	<.01	ACTUALLY	<.01
TONSILS	<.01	ADAMS	<.01
TOOL	<.01	AFFORD	<.01
TOOLS	<.01	AGE	<.01
TORN	<.01	AID	<.01
TRAINING	<.01	AIM	<.01
TRIMMED	<.01	AIRCRAFT	<.01
TRUNK	<.01	AIRPORT	<.01
TRUNKS	<.01	AISLE	<.01
TURKEYS	<.01	AJAX	<.01
TUXEDO	<.01	AL	<.01
TWINKIE	<.01	ALBERT	<.01
UNDERWEAR	<.01	ALIKE	<.01
UNLOCKS	<.01	ALLAN	<.01
UNTAG*	<.01	ALLOWANCES	<.01
VAMPIRE	<.01	ALPHABET	<.01
VERONICA	<.01	AMERICAN	<.01
WANDA	<.01	ANNIE	<.01
WARMER	<.01	ANTELOPE	<.01
WASTE	<.01	ANYBODY'S	<.01
WATCHES	<.01	ANYWAYS*	<.01
WATER'S	<.01	APOLLO	<.01
WATERFALL	<.01	APOLOGIZE	<.01
WEASELS	<.01	APPLESAUCE	<.01
WEBBED	<.01	AQUA	<.01
WEDDLE	<.01	ARCHERY	<.01

WORD	PERCENT	WORD	PERCENT
ARGUMENT	<.01	BON	<.01
ARMSTRONG'S	<.01	BONK	<.01
ARREST	<.01	BOOP*	<.01
ASTRONAUT	<.01	BOOT	<.01
ATARI	<.01	BOTHERING	<.01
AUNTS	<.01	BOTHERS	<.01
AUTO	<.01	BOUNCY	<.01
AUTOGRAPH	<.01	BOWLING	<.01
AX	<.01	BOYFRIENDS	<.01
BACKED	<.01	BRAND	<.01
BACKS	<.01	BRAUN	<.01
BADDER*	<.01	BRAVE	<.01
BAKER	<.01	BRAVER	<.01
BAKERY	<.01	BRAVEST	<.01
BALLENGER	<.01	BREATHE	<.01
BAND	<.01	BRENDA	<.01
BANDAID	<.01	BRENT	<.01
BARBARA	<.01	BRETT	<.01
BARBIE'S	<.01	BRIAN'S	<.01
BAREFOOTED	<.01	BROWNS	<.01
BBS	<.01	BUCKS	<.01
BEAGLE	<.01	BUFFY	<.01
BEAM	<.01	BUGGING	<.01
BEARD	<.01	BUGGY	<.01
BEASTIE	<.01	BULL	<.01
BECAME	<.01	BUMBLE	<.01
BEEF	<.01	BUNKER	<.01
BEEPS	<.01	BUNT	<.01
BEG	<.01	BURGLARS	<.01
BEGINS	<.01	BURNT	<.01
BELLE	<.01	BURT	<.01
BELT'S	<.01	BUTTERFLIES	<.01
BENCH	<.01	BUYING	<.01
BENCHES	<.01	CABLE	<.01
BENGALS	<.01	CACKLEBURG	<.01
BENJAMIN	<.01	CAMELS	<.01
BERETS	<.01	CANADA	<.01
BESSIE	<.01	CANDLE	<.01
BESTEST*	<.01	CANDLES	<.01
BIRDIES	<.01	CAPS	<.01
BITING	<.01	CAPSULE	<.01
BLACKHAWKS	<.01	CAREY	<.01
BLANK	<.01	CARL	<.01
BLANKETS	<.01	CAROLYN	<.01
BLINDFOLD	<.01	CARRIAGE	<.01
BLINDFOLDED	<.01	CART	<.01
BLOB	<.01	CASCADE	<.01
BLOCKING	<.01	CASES	<.01
BOARDWALK	<.01	CASPER'S	<.01
BOBBY'S	<.01	CASS	<.01

WORD	PERCENT	WORD	PERCENT
CAVITIES	<.01	CRAWDAD	<.01
CB	<.01	CRAWL	<.01
CB'S	<.01	CRAWLER	<.01
CELEBRATED	<.01	CRAWLERS	<.01
CHA	<.01	CRAWLS	<.01
CHAD	<.01	CREATURE	<.01
CHAINED	<.01	CREEPING	<.01
CHAINS	<.01	CRICKETS	<.01
CHALMER	<.01	CRISPY	<.01
CHAMPION	<.01	CROCODILE	<.01
CHAMPIONS	<.01	CROOK	<.01
CHAPS	<.01	CROWD	<.01
CHARGE	<.01	CRUSHED	<.01
CHEEP	<.01	CUCKOO	<.01
CHEERIOS	<.01	CUDDLY	<.01
CHEW	<.01	CUPCAKES	<.01
CHEWED	<.01	CURVE	<.01
CHIMFANZINE *	<.01	CURVED	<.01
CHIMNEYS	<.01	CURVES	<.01
CHINESE	<.01	CUSHIONS	<.01
CHIPPER	<.01	CUTS	<.01
CHOKING	<.01	CUTTED*	<.01
CHOP	<.01	DADDIES	<.01
CHORES	<.01	DAISIES	<.01
CHOSEN	<.01	DAKOTA	<.01
CIGARETTE	<.01	DANG	<.01
CINDY'S	<.01	DARTH	<.01
CLIP	<.01	DAUGHTERS	<.01
CLUBHOUSE	<.01	DAVE	<.01
CLUBS	<.01	DAVIS	<.01
COACH'S	<.01	DEAF	<.01
COAL	<.01	DEAL	<.01
COIN	<.01	DEAN	<.01
COMFORTABLE	<.01	DEANN	<.01
COMMUNITY	<.01	DECIDE	<.01
COMPACTOR	<.01	DECKS	<.01
COMPETING	<.01	DECORATION	<.01
CONNIE	<.01	DELCO	<.01
CONTEST	<.01	DENISE	<.01
CONTINUED	<.01	DESERT	<.01
CONTROLS	<.01	DETECTIVE	<.01
COO	<.01	DIAGONAL	<.01
COOKIE'S	<.01	DIANE'S	<.01
COOPER	<.01	DIET	<.01
CORVETTE	<.01	DIFFERENCE	<.01
COSTS	<.01	DINOSAUR'S	<.01
COUCHES	<.01	DIP	<.01
COURTS	<.01	DIPPER	<.01
CRACKER	<.01	DIRECTION	<.01
CRAIG	<.01	DIRECTIONS	<.01

WORD	PERCENT	WORD	PERCENT
DISGUISE	<.01	FAULT	<.01
DITCH	<.01	FEATHERS	<.01
DIVORCED	<.01	FEELED*	<.01
DIXON	<.01	FEELING	<.01
DIZZY	<.01	FENCES	<.01
DOCTOR'S	<.01	FINGERNAIL	<.01
DODGE	<.01	FIRETRUCK	<.01
DODGER	<.01	FIRING	<.01
DOE	<.01	FIXES	<.01
DOLLIES	<.01	FLIPPING	<.01
DONED*	<.01	FLOODED	<.01
DONNOR	<.01	FLOORS	<.01
DOORBELL	<.01	FLOPPING	<.01
DOROTHY'S	<.01	FLOUR	<.01
DOUGIE	<.01	FLUNK	<.01
DRAIN	<.01	FOLD	<.01
DREW	<.01	FOREVER	<.01
DRIVED*	<.01	FORGETTING	<.01
DROWNS	<.01	FORT	<.01
DRUM	<.01	FOSSIL	<.01
DUDE	<.01	FOWLER	<.01
DUMMIES	<.01	FRACTURED	<.01
DUNKED	<.01	FREAK	<.01
DUST	<.01	FRED'S	<.01
DYNAMUTT	<.01	FRITZIE	<.01
EARL	<.01	FRONTWARDS	<.01
EARTH	<.01	FURTHER	<.01
EARTHQUAKE	<.01	FUZZY	<.01
EATER	<.01	GALLERY	<.01
EGGHEAD	<.01	GARFIELD	<.01
EIGHTH	<.01	GARGOYLE	<.01
EIGHTS	<.01	GARTER	<.01
ELASTIC	<.01	GARY	<.01
ELBOW	<.01	GATES	<.01
ELMER	<.01	GATHERED	<.01
ELWOOD	<.01	GEE	<.01
EMPTY	<.01	GENTLY	<.01
ENDS	<.01	GIDDY	<.01
ENJOY	<.01	GIZZARD	<.01
ERIC'S	<.01	GNIP-GNOP	<.01
ERICKSON	<.01	GOBBLE	<.01
ERN	<.01	GOBBLED	<.01
ESTHER'S	<.01	GODZILLAS	<.01
EVENING	<.01	GOED*	<.01
EXCITED	<.01	GOLDMAN	<.01
EXPERIMENT	<.01	GOOCHIE	<.01
EXTRA	<.01	GOODEST*	<.01
FACING	<.01	GOODS	<.01
FAINTED	<.01	GORDON'S	<.01
FARMERS	<.01	GRABS	<.01

WORD	PERCENT	WORD	PERCENT
GRANDPAS	<.01	HOLLY'S	<.01
GRANNY	<.01	HOMEWORK	<.01
GRAVEL	<.01	HOOTCHIE	<.01
GRAYS	<.01	HORNER	<.01
GRENADES	<.01	HOSES	<.01
GRINDED*	<.01	HOST	<.01
GRINNING	<.01	HOTDOGS	<.01
GROSS	<.01	HOTELS	<.01
GROVER'S	<.01	HOW'D	<.01
GROWLING	<.01	HUGGING	<.01
GUARD	<.01	HULK	<.01
GUARDING	<.01	HUNK	<.01
GUESSED	<.01	HUSKER	<.01
GUESSES	<.01	ICES	<.01
GUIDE	<.01	INFECTION	<.01
GUMDROPS	<.01	INVESTIGATION	<.01
GYPSY	<.01	INVITATION	<.01
HADN'T	<.01	INVITE	<.01
HAINES	<.01	ISRAEL	<.01
HALVES	<.01	JACKPOT	<.01
HAMBURGERS	<.01	JACKS	<.01
HAMSTER	<.01	JACOB	<.01
HANDOFF	<.01	JAILS	<.01
HAPPILY	<.01	JAM	<.01
HARDER	<.01	JASON'S	<.01
HARPOONS	<.01	JEANNIE	<.01
HATCHED	<.01	JED'S	<.01
HATCHET	<.01	JELLO	<.01
HAUS	<.01	JIM'S	<.01
HAYRIDE	<.01	JIMMY'S	<.01
HAYSTACK	<.01	JOHNSON	<.01
HEART'S	<.01	JOIN	<.01
HEATHER'S	<.01	JOKER'S	<.01
HEATING	<.01	JUNGLE	<.01
HEELS	<.01	KEEPING	<.01
HEIGHTS	<.01	KELLY'S	<.01
HELD	<.01	KENOBI	<.01
HENS	<.01	KERMIT	<.01
HERO	<.01	KEYS	<.01
HIBERNATE	<.01	KIM'S	<.01
HICCUP	<.01	KINGED	<.01
HIDEOUT	<.01	KIT	<.01
HIGHCHAIR	<.01	KITE	<.01
HIGHWAY	<.01	KLEENEX	<.01
HILDA	<.01	KNIGHTS	<.01
HILLSIDE	<.01	KNOT	<.01
HILLY	<.01	KNOTS	<.01
HIVE	<.01	KOOTCHIE	<.01
HOGAN	<.01	KYGER	<.01
HOLLOW	<.01	LASSIE'S	<.01

WORD	PERCENT	WORD	PERCENT
LAURA'S	<.01	METS	<.01
LAURIE'S	<.01	MID	<.01
LAVA	<.01	MILWAUKEE	<.01
LAW	<.01	MINDS	<.01
LAZY	<.01	MISSIONS	<.01
LEAFS	<.01	MISSOURI	<.01
LEAKS	<.01	MISTRESS	<.01
LED	<.01	MITCHELL	<.01
LEFTOVER	<.01	MIXER	<.01
LEGAL	<.01	MOLLY	<.01
LEIA	<.01	MONSON	<.01
LENNY	<.01	MOOSE	<.01
LEOPARDS	<.01	MOP	<.01
LESS	<.01	MORTON	<.01
LIE	<.01	MOSES	<.01
LIMBS	<.01	MOUNTIE	<.01
LIZARDS	<.01	MOUTHS	<.01
LIZZIE	<.01	MOW	<.01
LOAD	<.01	MOWER	<.01
LOAF	<.01	MUDDY	<.01
LOBBY	<.01	MUGGS	<.01
LOBSTER	<.01	MUPPET	<.01
LOCKS	<.01	MUPPETS	<.01
LOLLIPOP	<.01	MUSCLES	<.01
LONGEST	<.01	MUSH	<.01
LOSERS	<.01	MYTHS	<.01
LOUDER	<.01	NAILS	<.01
LOUIS	<.01	NAPS	<.01
LOUISVILLE	<.01	NATURE	<.01
LUCK	<.01	NEEDLES	<.01
LUCKILY	<.01	NERF	<.01
LUMPY	<.01	NEWEST	<.01
MA	<.01	NEWTON	<.01
MAC	<.01	NINA	<.01
MADED*	<.01	NOBODY'S	<.01
MAIN	<.01	NOSEY	<.01
MAKED*	<.01	NOTHING'S	<.01
MAPLECREST	<.01	NOTICE	<.01
MARRY	<.01	NOTICED	<.01
MASON	<.01	O'S	<.01
MATCHING	<.01	OATMEAL	<.01
MATE	<.01	OFFS	<.01
MATINEE	<.01	OLDS	<.01
MEANT	<.01	OPERATE	<.01
MEETING	<.01	OPPONENT	<.01
MEETS	<.01	OTTO	<.01
MEGALON	<.01	OWE	<.01
MELTS	<.01	OWNS	<.01
MESSING	<.01	OXYGEN	<.01
MESSY	<.01	PACKING	<.01

WORD	PERCENT	WORD	PERCENT
PADDLES	<.01	PORCUPINE	<.01
PAIN	<.01	PORRIDGES	<.01
PAINTBRUSH	<.01	POSSUM'S	<.01
PAINTINGS	<.01	POSTS	<.01
PALS	<.01	POTS	<.01
PAMPA	<.01	POTTERY	<.01
PANS	<.01	POURED	<.01
PAPILLON	<.01	POURING	<.01
PARK'S	<.01	POWDER	<.01
PARKING	<.01	POX	<.01
PASSES	<.01	PRAIRIE	<.01
PASSWORD	<.01	PRESTON	<.01
PAT	<.01	PRETZEL	<.01
PAVILLION	<.01	PREVIEWS	<.01
PECKED	<.01	PRICE	<.01
PEDALS	<.01	PRINCES	<.01
PEG	<.01	PRINCIPAL	<.01
PENNY	<.01	PRINTS	<.01
PENNY'S	<.01	PRIVACY	<.01
PERFUME	<.01	PROMISE	<.01
PERRY	<.01	PROPERTIES	<.01
PETTING	<.01	PROUD	<.01
PHANTOM	<.01	PUFFS	<.01
PICNICS	<.01	PUNCHED	<.01
PIER	<.01	PUNCHES	<.01
PILGRIMS	<.01	QUEENIE	<.01
PINBALL	<.01	QUICKLY	<.01
PINOPLY*	<.01	QUIZMO	<.01
PINS	<.01	RACED	<.01
PINTS	<.01	RACK	<.01
PIPES	<.01	RACKO	<.01
PIRATES	<.01	RADAR	<.01
PISTOL	<.01	RAINY	<.01
PIZZAS	<.01	RALLY	<.01
PLAINTS	<.01	RATHER	<.01
PLANS	<.01	RAW	<.01
PLANTED	<.01	RAYMOND	<.01
PLAYMATE	<.01	REAR	<.01
PLEEZERS*	<.01	REBECCA	<.01
PLUMBING	<.01	REDDER	<.01
POHLMAN'S	<.01	REDSKINS	<.01
POINTED	<.01	REFEREES	<.01
POKE	<.01	REFUSE	<.01
POLES	<.01	REGGIE	<.01
POLICES*	<.01	REINDEER'S	<.01
PONG	<.01	RENA	<.01
PONYTAIL	<.01	RERUN	<.01
POOF	<.01	RESCUED	<.01
POPEYE'S	<.01	RHINOCEROS	<.01
POPPING	<.01	RICE	<.01

WORD	PERCENT	WORD	PERCENT
RICHIE'S	<.01	SEARS	<.01
RIDDLER	<.01	SEASHORE	<.01
RIFLES	<.01	SEASICK	<.01
RISK	<.01	SECONDS	<.01
ROADS	<.01	SEEM	<.01
ROBBER'S	<.01	SENSES	<.01
ROBBIE	<.01	SERVING	<.01
ROBOT'S	<.01	SETTED*	<.01
ROCK-A-BYE	<.01	SETTLE	<.01
ROCK'EM	<.01	SEVENS	<.01
ROCKVILLE	<.01	SEVENTH	<.01
RODEO	<.01	SEWER	<.01
ROMAIN	<.01	SEWING	<.01
ROOFS	<.01	SHAKED	<.01
ROOKIES	<.01	SHAKING	<.01
ROOSTERS	<.01	SHARPEN	<.01
ROSS	<.01	SHARPER	<.01
ROUNDS	<.01	SHED	<.01
ROUTE	<.01	SHELLY'S	<.01
RUBBLE	<.01	SHELVES	<.01
RUGS	<.01	SHEPHERDS	<.01
RUIN	<.01	SHIELD	<.01
RUST	<.01	SHOED	<.01
RYE	<.01	SHOPPED	<.01
SABRINA	<.01	SHOULDER	<.01
SAFETY	<.01	SHY	<.01
SAILBOAT	<.01	SIDETRACK	<.01
SAILBOATS	<.01	SIDEWALKS	<.01
SAILED	<.01	SIGMUND	<.01
SAN	<.01	SIGMUNDS	<.01
SANDALS	<.01	SILENT	<.01
SANDBOX	<.01	SILVERWARE	<.01
SANDRA	<.01	SISSY	<.01
SAVER	<.01	SIXES	<.01
SCARECROW'S	<.01	SIXTEENTH	<.01
SCATTERED	<.01	SKATED	<.01
SCIENTIST	<.01	SKID	<.01
SCISSORS	<.01	SKILL	<.01
SCOTCH	<.01	SKUNK'S	<.01
SCOUT	<.01	SKUNKS	<.01
SCRAMBLE	<.01	SKYWALKER	<.01
SCRAMBLER	<.01	SLAMMED	<.01
SCRAP	<.01	SLEDDING	<.01
SCRAPER	<.01	SLEEVE	<.01
SCRATCH	<.01	SLIDED*	<.01
SCRATCHES	<.01	SLIMY	<.01
SCREEN	<.01	SLINGSHOT	<.01
SCREWS	<.01	SLIPPING	<.01
SCROOGE	<.01	SLIPS	<.01
SCRUFFY	<.01	SLUG*	<.01

WORD	PERCENT	WORD	PERCENT
SLUGS	<.01	STEVE'S	<.01
SMACK	<.01	STINGED*	<.01
SMACKS	<.01	STINKS	<.01
SMARTER	<.01	STOMPING	<.01
SMASHING	<.01	STONE	<.01
SMILES	<.01	STRAP	<.01
SMOOTH	<.01	STRAWBERRIES	<.01
SMURF	<.01	STRAWBERRY	<.01
SMURFS	<.01	STREAM	<.01
SNAP	<.01	STRINGS	<.01
SNAPPED	<.01	STRUT	<.01
SNORKEL	<.01	STUNG	<.01
SNOWCONE	<.01	SUFFOCATE	<.01
SNOWMOBILE	<.01	SUITCASE	<.01
SNUCK*	<.01	SUMMERTIME	<.01
SNUCKED*	<.01	SUNBURNED	<.01
SOAKED	<.01	SUNSHINE	<.01
SOLDIER'S	<.01	SUZY	<.01
SOLID	<.01	SWAMMED	<.01
SOLVE	<.01	SWEATY	<.01
SOMEDAY	<.01	SWEEPING	<.01
SOMEONES*	<.01	SWINGED*	<.01
SONNY	<.01	SWIPED	<.01
SPACEMAN	<.01	SWITCHES	<.01
SPACESHIP	<.01	SWUNG	<.01
SPAGHETTI	<.01	SYRUP	<.01
SPANKS	<.01	TABLES	<.01
SPARE	<.01	TACKLING	<.01
SPEAKED*	<.01	TAGGING	<.01
SPECIALS	<.01	TANGLED	<.01
SPEEDING	<.01	TAPES	<.01
SPEEDWAY	<.01	TATTLE	<.01
SPELLED	<.01	TEACHED*	<.01
SPELLS	<.01	TEACHES	<.01
SPENDED*	<.01	TEAPOT	<.01
SPIDERMAN'S	<.01	TENTH	<.01
SPITTING	<.01	TESTS	<.01
SPLIT	<.01	TEXAS	<.01
SPOKES	<.01	THAT'LL	<.01
·SPRAYS	<.01	THEM'S*	<.01
SPUN	<.01	THEY'D	<.01
SPY	<.01	THREAD	<.01
SQUASH	<.01	THUNDER	<.01
SQUEEZED	<.01	TIDAL	<.01
STADIUM	<.01	TIGGER'S	<.01
STALKER	<.01	TIP	<.01
STAPLE	<.01	TIPPED	<.01
STATIONS	<.01	TOAD	<.01
STATUES	<.01	TOMATOES	<.01
STEELERS	<.01	TONTO	<.01

WORD	PERCENT	WORD	PERCENT
TORNADOES	<.01	WEIGH	<.01
TOTTER	<.01	WELBY	<.01
TOW	<.01	WHATCHAMACALLIT	<.01
TOWEL	<.01	WHEELBARROW	<.01
TOWELS	<.01	WHIFF	<.01
TOWER'S	<.01	WHISPERED	<.01
TRACTOR	<.01	WHITISH	<.01
TRACY'S	<.01	WHOOP	<.01
TRAILS	<.01	WIDOW	<.01
TRAMPOLINE	<.01	WIFES*	<.01
TREK'S	<.01	WIGS	<.01
TRICYCLE	<.01	WILLIAMSON	<.01
TRIPLE	<.01	WINDING	<.01
TROPHY	<.01	WING	<.01
TROT	<.01	WINNED*	<.01
TROUBLES	<.01	WISE	<.01
TUBES	<.01	WITCH'S	<.01
TURNER	<.01	WOLFMAN	<.01
TWEETY	<.01	WOMEN	<.01
TWENTY-FOUR	<.01	WONDERED	<.01
TWENTY-SEVEN	<.01	WORKBOOK	<.01
TWENTY-THREE	<.01	WORSER*	<.01
TWIRLS	<.01	WORTH	<.01
TY	<.01	WRAP	<.01
TYLER'S	<.01	WRAPPER	<.01
TYPEWRITE	<.01	WRAPPING	<.01
UMBRELLA	<.01	WRIST	<.01
UMPIRE	<.01	Y	<.01
UNCLES	<.01	YACKO	<.01
UNLOCKED	<.01	YAHTZEES	<.01
UTAH	<.01	YOGI'S	<.01
VADER	<.01	YORK	<.01
VALENTINE'S	<.01	YUCK	<.01
VALLEY	<.01	YUCKY	<.01
VERSES	<.01	YUM	<.01
VEST	<.01	ZACK	<.01
VINEGAR	<.01	ZOOS	<.01
VINTON	<.01	ACCOMPLISH	<.01
VISITOR	<.01	ACCOUNT	<.01
VISITORS	<.01	ACES	<.01
VISITS	<.01	ACROBATERS*	<.01
VOLCANO	<.01	ACTIVITY	<.01
WAFFLE	<.01	AD	<.01
WALKIE-TALKIE	<.01	ADDED	<.01
WALLACE	<.01	ADDING	<.01
WALTONS	<.01	ADRIAN'S	<.01
WASHERS	<.01	ADVENTURE	<.01
WASP	<.01	AFFAIR	<.01
WEAK	<.01	AFGHAN	<.01
WEENY	<.01	AFTERNOONS	<.01

WORD	PERCENT	WORD	PERCENT
AGENTS	<.01	BARGAIN	<.01
AIMED	<.01	BARNABY	<.01
ALARMS	<.01	BARNYARD	<.01
ALASKA	<.01	BARON	<.01
ALICIA	<.01	BARRELS	<.01
ALTOGETHER	<.01	BARREN	<.01
AMAZING	<.01	BARRY	<.01
AMMUNITION	<.01	BASEBALL'S	<.01
AMUSEMENT	<.01	BASKIN	<.01
ANITA	<.01	BASS	<.01
ANN'S	<.01	BATHROOMS	<.01
ANTENNAS	<.01	BATHS	<.01
ANTHONY	<.01	BATON	<.01
ANYHOW	<.01	BATTED	<.01
APOLOGIZED	<.01	BATTERS	<.01
APRON	<.01	BATTERY	<.01
AQUARIUM	<.01	BAWLING	<.01
AQUARIUS	<.01	BEA'S	<.01
ARGUED	<.01	BEADS	<.01
ARK	<.01	BEAK	<.01
ARM'S	<.01	BEAST	<.01
ARRESTS	<.01	BEATEN	<.01
ARTIE	<.01	BEAUTY	<.01
ASLEEPS*	<.01	BEAVERS	<.01
ASSOCIATED	<.01	BEAZLEY	<.01
ATARIS	<.01	BED'S	<.01
ATLANTA	<.01	BEDTIME	<.01
ATTACHED	<.01	BEEHIVE	<.01
ATTACKED	<.01	BEEHIVES	<.01
ATTENTION	<.01	BEESWAX	<.01
AUCTION	<.01	BEGAN	<.01
AUNTIE	<.01	BEGGED	<.01
AUTOBIOGRAPHY	<.01	BEGIN	<.01
AUTUMN	<.01	BEHINDS	<.01
BABYSITTED*	<.01	BEIGE	<.01
BABYSITTING	<.01	BEINGS	<.01
BACKPACK	<.01	BELCHER*	<.01
BACKWARD	<.01	BELIEVED	<.01
BADLANDS	<.01	BELIEVES	<.01
BAGGIE	<.01	BELINDA	<.01
BALLETS	<.01	BELLYACHE	<.01
BAM	<.01	BEN'S	<.01
BANDITS	<.01	BENDING	<.01
BANGED	<.01	BENEATH	<.01
BANGING	<.01	BERRIES	<.01
BANGS	<.01	BERT	<.01
BANKER	<.01	BESIDES	<.01
BARBER	<.01	BETH	<.01
BARE	<.01	BETTED	<.01
BAREFOOT	<.01	BEVINGTON	<.01

WORD	PERCENT	WORD	PERCENT
BIDDLE	<.01	BOWL'S	<.01
BIGFOOTS	<.01	BOWS	<.01
BIGS*	<.01	BRACES	<.01
BILL'S	<.01	BRAID	<.01
BILLFOLD	<.01	BRAIDED	<.01
BINGOS	<.01	BRAIDS	<.01
BIOGRAPHY	<.01	BRANDON	<.01
BIRD'S	<.01	BRANDY	<.01
BIRDSEED	<.01	BREAKED*	<.01
BIRTH	<.01	BREATH	<.01
BIRTHSTONE	<.01	BRETT'S	<.01
BITED	<.01	BRIANS	<.01
BITS	<.01	BRICKED	<.01
BLACKBIRDS	<.01	BRITCHES	<.01
BLACKBOARD	<.01	BROKES*	<.01
BLACKS	<.01	BRONCHITIS	<.01
BLAME	<.01	BRONTOSAURUS	<.01
BLANKS	<.01	BROOK'S	<.01
BLAZE	<.01	BROOKIE	<.01
BLEACHERS	<.01	BROOKS	<.01
BLESS	<.01	BROWNISH	<.01
BLIND	<.01	BROWS	<.01
BLINKING	<.01	BRUCE	<.01
BLOCKAGE	<.01	BRUSHED	<.01
BLOCKED	<.01	BRUSHES	<.01
BLOCKHEAD	<.01	BRUSHING	<.01
BLOOMING	<.01	BRUTUS'	<.01
BLOWN	<.01	BUBBLY	<.01
BLUEJEANS	<.01	BUCK'S	<.01
BLUFF	<.01	BUCKLED	<.01
BLUISH	<.01	BUDDING	<.01
BLUSHING	<.01	BUILDS	<.01
BLUSTERY	<.01	BULBS	<.01
BOBS	<.01	BULL'S-EYE	<.01
BODY'S	<.01	BUM	<.01
BOIL	<.01	BUMPING	<.01
BOLD	<.01	BUMS	<.01
BOLT	<.01	BUNCHES	<.01
BOMBER	<.01	BUNNY'S	<.01
BONEMAN	<.01	BURNEDED	<.01
BONNET	<.01	BURNS	<.01
BOOMED	<.01	BURRO	<.01
BOOTH	<.01	BURST	<.01
BORED	<.01	BUSCH	<.01
BORROWED	<.01	BUSSES	<.01
BOSLEY	<.01	BUSTING	<.01
BOSTON	<.01	BUSTS	<.01
BOTHER	<.01	BUTS	<.01
BOUNDS	<.01	BUYED*	<.01
BOUT	<.01	CABANA	<.01

WORD	PERCENT	WORD	PERCENT
CABINETS	<.01	CHARGING	<.01
CACTUS	<.01	CHARLENE	<.01
CADILLAC	<.01	CHART	<.01
CAFETERIA	<.01	CHASERS	<.01
CAIN	<.01	CHATTERING	<.01
CALF	<.01	CHEATED	<.01
CAMERAS	<.01	CHEATING	<.01
CAMPGROUND	<.01	CHECKMATE	<.01
CANARY	<.01	CHEEPIES	<.01
CANE	<.01	CHERYL	<.01
CANNED	<.01	CHESTS	<.01
CANNOT	<.01	CHEVY	<.01
CANTEEN	<.01	CHEWBACCA	<.01
CAPER	<.01	CHICKEN'S	<.01
CAPITALS	<.01	CHILD'S	<.01
CARBURETOR	<.01	CHILLER	<.01
CARDINALS	<.01	CHIMPANZEE	<.01
CAREERS	<.01	CHINA'S	<.01
CARIBBEAN	<.01	CHIPMUNK	<.01
CARLSBAD	<.01	CHIPPED	<.01
CARNIVAL	<.01	CHOICE	<.01
CARNIVALS	<.01	CHOICES	<.01
CARP	<.01	CHOMP	<.01
CARPENTER	<.01	CHOO-CHOO	<.01
CARRIE	<.01	CHRISTA	<.01
CARRIER	<.01	CHUCKIE'S	<.01
CARTER	<.01	CHUGGY	<.01
CARVED	<.01	CHUM	<.01
CASH	<.01	CHUNKS	<.01
CASTOR	<.01	CIGARS	<.01
CATCHER'S	<.01	CINCH	<.01
CATERPILLAR	<.01	CINCO	<.01
CATHERINE	<.01	CIRCUSES	<.01
CAUSING	<.01	CITIES	<.01
CAVED	<.01	CLARA	<.01
CAVEMEN	<.01	CLASS'	<.01
CAVERNS	<.01	CLAWS	<.01
CBS	<.01	CLEANER	<.01
CC	<.01	CLEANS	<.01
CEDAR	<.01	CLEATS	<.01
CELERY	<.01	CLIFFS	<.01
CEMENTY*	<.01	CLIPS	<.01
CHAMP	<.01	CLOCKS	<.01
CHAMPAIGN	<.01	CLOGS	<.01
CHANGES	<.01	CLOSES	<.01
CHANNELS	<.01	CLOTHER'S	<.01
CHAPMAN	<.01	CLOUDY	<.01
CHAR	<.01	CLUCK	<.01
CHARADES	<.01	CLUNKED	<.01
CHARGED	<.01	COACHES	<.01

WORD	PERCENT	WORD	PERCENT
COCA-COLA	<.01	CRABBY	<.01
COCKER	<.01	CRACKS	<.01
COFFIN	<.01	CRANE	<.01
COLE	<.01	CRANK	<.01
COLGATE	<.01	CRAPPIE	<.01
COLLAPSED	<.01	CRAPPY	<.01
COLLAPSES	<.01	CRASHES	<.01
COLLARS	<.01	CRASHING	<.01
COLLEEN	<.01	CRAWDADS	<.01
COLLEEN'S	<.01	CRAYFISH	<.01
COLONIAL	<.01	CRAZIEST	<.01
COLTRAIN	<.01	CREAM'S	<.01
COLTS	<.01	CREATES	<.01
COLUMBIAN	<.01	CREEP	<.01
COLUMBUS	<.01	CREEPED*	<.01
COLUMY	<.01	CREPT	<.01
COMANCHE	<.01	CRIMINALS	<.01
COMETS	<.01	CRITTERS	<.01
COMIC	<.01	CROAK	<.01
COMMAND	<.01	CROSSED	<.01
COMMANDERS	<.01	CROSSES	<.01
COMMUNION	<.01	CROSSINGS	<.01
COMPARED	<.01	CROWDED	<.01
COMPETITION	<.01	CRUEL	<.01
CONCESSION	<.01	CRUISER	<.01
CONDUCTOR	<.01	CRUMBLE	<.01
CONFERENCE	<.01	CRUNCH	<.01
CONK	<.01	CRUNCHED	<.01
CONTACT	<.01	CRUSHES	<.01
CONTAINER	<.01	CRYSTALS	<.01
CONTEMPORARY	<.01	CUB	<.01
CONTESTS	<.01	CUDDLES	<.01
CONTINUE	<.01	CUFFS	<.01
CONTRAPTION	<.01	CURE	<.01
CONTROLLING	<.01	CURIOUS	<.01
CONVERSATION	<.01	CURLING	<.01
COOKER	<.01	CURSED	<.01
COOKOUTS	<.01	CURSES	<.01
COOLS	<.01	CURVING	<.01
COONS	<.01	CURVY*	<.01
CORD	<.01	CUSS	<.01
COREY	<.01	CUSSES	<.01
CORKY'S	<.01	DABA	<.01
CORNY	<.01	DAG NABBIT	<.01
CORPMAN	<.01	DAILY	<.01
CORRECTING	<.01	DAISY'S	<.01
CORRIE	<.01	DANCER'S	<.01
COUGH	<.01	DANIELLE	<.01
COUNTER	<.01	DAPHNE	<.01
COWARD	<.01	DAR	<.01

WORD	PERCENT	WORD	PERCENT
DARBY	<.01	DOMES	<.01
DARE	<.01	DONNA'S	<.01
DARKEST	<.01	DOO'S	<.01
DARLA	<.01	DOOBY	<.01
DARLENE	<.01	DOORWAY'S	<.01
DARLING	<.01	DOREENA	<.01
DARYL	<.01	DOS	<.01
DATE	<.01	DOT'S	<.01
DAVE'S	<.01	DOUBLES	<.01
DAVID'S	<.01	DOUBLING	<.01
DAVIDSON	<.01	DOVE	<.01
DEACT*	<.01	DOWNED	<.01
DEALER	<.01	DOZEN	<.01
DEARS	<.01	DOZENS	<.01
DEATH	<.01	DRACULA'S	<.01
DECISION	<.01	DRAGGED	<.01
DECORATED	<.01	DRAGGING	<.01
DEED	<.01	DRAGONS	<.01
DEERS*	<.01	DRAPERIES	<.01
DEFENSE	<.01	DRAPES	<.01
DEFFENBAUGH	<.01	DRAWERS	<.01
DEGREES	<.01	DRAWS	<.01
DELANEY	<.01	DREAMS	<.01
DELIRIOUS	<.01	DREWED*	<.01
DENTED	<.01	DRIBBLE	<.01
DEPENDS	<.01	DRIES	<.01
DEPUTY	<.01	DRILL	<.01
DERRICK	<.01	DRIPS	<.01
DESIGNS	<.01	DRUMMER	<.01
DESKSTAR	<.01	DRYWALL	<.01
DESSERT	<.01	DUB	<.01
DESTROYER	<.01	DUCK'S	<.01
DESTROYS	<.01	DUCKER*	<.01
DEVILS	<.01	DUCKIES	<.01
DEVLIN	<.01	DUCKING	<.01
DIARY	<.01	DUEL	<.01
DILLY	<.01	DUGOUT	<.01
DINGS	<.01	DULUTH	<.01
DINKY	<.01	DUMBEST	<.01
DISGUISED	<.01	DUMPED	<.01
DISHWASHER	<.01	DUMPING	<.01
DISNEY'S	<.01	DUNK	<.01
DITTY	<.01	DWARFS*	<.01
DIVER	<.01	EAGLES	<.01
DIVERS	<.01	EARPHONES	<.01
DIVISION	<.01	EARRING	<.01
DOCTORS	<.01	EARRINGS	<.01
DODGEBALL	<.01	EASIER	<.01
DOGGIE'S	<.01	EAST	<.01
DOME'S	<.01	EBBIE	<.01

WORD	PERCENT	WORD	PERCENT
EDDIE	<.01	FANTASY	<.01
EELS	<.01	FARAH	<.01
EGGROLLS	<.01	FARMS	<.01
ELEVATORS	<.01	FARTHEST	<.01
ELEVENTH	<.01	FARTS	<.01
ELLA	<.01	FASHIONED	<.01
ELLEN	<.01	FASTBALL	<.01
ELZROTH	<.01	FASTEN	<.01
ELZROTH'S	<.01	FATSO	<.01
EMBARRASSED	<.01	FATTER	<.01
EMMA	<.01	FATTY	<.01
EMPIRE	<.01	FAUCET	<.01
ENEMIES	<.01	FAWCETT	<.01
ENGINES	<.01	FEATHERY	<.01
ENVELOPE	<.01	FEELINGS	<.01
EQUALS	<.01	FEETS*	<.01
ERASERS	<.01	FELIX	<.01
ERUPTED	<.01	FELLOW	<.01
ESP	<.01	FETCH	<.01
EVERYONE'S	<.01	FIB	<.01
EVIDENTLY	<.01	FICTION	<.01
EVIL	<.01	FIFTEENTH	<.01
EXCITE	<.01	FIFTIES	<.01
EXCITINGEST*	<.01	FIGURED	<.01
EXERCISE	<.01	FIGURES	<.01
EXERCISES	<.01	FILES	<.01
EXIST	<.01	FILLS	<.01
EXPEDITION	<.01	FIN	<.01
EXPENSIVE	<.01	FINDED*	<.01
EXPLODES	<.01	FINISHES	<.01
EXPLORE	<.01	FIREBALL	<.01
EXTINGUISH	<.01	FIREMAN'S	<.01
EXTRAS	<.01	FIREPLACES	<.01
EYEBALLS	<.01	FIRES	<.01
EYEBROWS	<.01	FIRETRUCKS	<.01
EYEGLASS	<.01	FIREWORKS	<.01
EYEGLASSES	<.01	FIRSTLY	<.01
EYELIDS	<.01	FIST	<.01
FACED	<.01	FITTED	<.01
FACT	<.01	FIVES	<.01
FAINTS	<.01	FLAMES	<.01
FAIRGROUND	<.01	FLAP	<.01
FAIRS	<.01	FLASHLIGHT	<.01
FAKES	<.01	FLAVOR	<.01
FAKING	<.01	FLEAS	<.01
FALLEN	<.01	FLING	<.01
FAMILY'S	<.01	FLINGED	<.01
FAMOUS	<.01	FLINTSTONES	<.01
FANCY	<.01	FLO	<.01
FANNING	<.01	FLOPPED	<.01

WORD	PERCENT	WORD	PERCENT
FLOPPY	<.01	GAUGE	<.01
FLOPS	<.01	GAZELLE	<.01
FLORA	<.01	GEAR	<.01
FLOWN	<.01	GENIE	<.01
FLOYD	<.01	GERMANY	<.01
FLU	<.01	GIGGLES	<.01
FLUSH	<.01	GIGGLING	<.01
FLUSHED	<.01	GINA'S	<.01
FLUTE	<.01	GIRLIE	<.01
FLYNN	<.01	GIVED*	<.01
FONZIE'S	<.01	GIVEN	<.01
FOOTBALL'S	<.01	GIZMO	<.01
FOOTBALLS	<.01	GLITTER	<.01
FORCED	<.01	GLORIA	<.01
FORKS	<.01	GLOW	<.01
FORM	<.01	GLOWS	<.01
FORWARDS	<.01	GLUES	<.01
FOSSILS	<.01	GNAW	<.01
FOUNDED*	<.01	GOBS	<.01
FOUNTAIN	<.01	GODFATHER	<.01
FOUNTAINS	<.01	GOINGED*	<.01
FOUR-NINETY-FIVE	<.01	GOOBER	<.01
FOXY	<.01	GOODER*	<.01
FRANCIS	<.01	GOOF	<.01
FRANCISCO	<.01	GOOFED	<.01
FRANK	<.01	GOOFING	<.01
FRANKFURTER	<.01	GOOFS	<.01
FREDDIE	<.01	GOONS	<.01
FREEZED*	<.01	GORDY	<.01
FREEZEMAN	<.01	GOVERNMENT	<.01
FREEZER	<.01	GRAD	<.01
FREIGHTERS	<.01	GRADES	<.01
FRIES	<.01	GRAM	<.01
FROGGIES	<.01	GRAMMAS	<.01
FROSTIES	<.01	GRAMPA'S	<.01
FRY	<.01	GRANDMAS	<.01
FUNERAL	<.01	GRANDPARENTS	<.01
FUNNER*	<.01	GRANGE	<.01
FURRY	<.01	GRAPE	<.01
FUSES	<.01	GRAPES	<.01
FUTURE	<.01	GRAYISH	<.01
FUZZ	<.01	GREASE	<.01
GAME'S	<.01	GREATER	<.01
GAR'S	<.01	GREENISH	<.01
GARAGES	<.01	GREENS	<.01
GARDENER	<.01	GREGS	<.01
GARDENERS	<.01	GRIFFIN	<.01
GARDENS	<.01	GRIND	<.01
GASOLINE	<.01	GROUNDED	<.01
GASTON	<.01	GROWL	<.01

WORD	PERCENT	WORD	PERCENT
GUARDS	<.01	HERD	<.01
GUESSING	<.01	HICCUPS	<.01
GUIDES	<.01	HIDDEN	<.01
GULF	<.01	HIDE-A-BED	<.01
GUMBALL	<.01	HIKED	<.01
GUNFIGHTS	<.01	HIND	<.01
GUNNY	<.01	HINKLE'S	<.01
GUNSMOKE	<.01	HINKLES	<.01
GUSTO	<.01	HIPPOS	<.01
GUTS	<.01	HIRE	<.01
GYMS	<.01	HIRES	<.01
HAIR'S	<.01	HITTED*	<.01
HAIRS	<.01	HOKEY-POKEY	<.01
HALFWAY	<.01	HOLDER	<.01
HALO	<.01	HOLDERS	<.01
HALTER	<.01	HOLIDAYS	<.01
HAND'S	<.01	HOLLAND	<.01
HANDCUFFS	<.01	HOLLERING	<.01
HANDLES	<.01	HOLLERS	<.01
HANESWORTH	<.01	HOLLYWOOD	<.01
HANGERS	<.01	HOLOCAUST	<.01
HANGS	<.01	HONESTY	<.01
HAPPENING	<.01	HONEYCOMBS	<.01
HAPPINESS	<.01	HONG	<.01
HARMONY	<.01	HOOK'S	<.01
HASWELL	<.01	HOOKEY	<.01
HATCHING	<.01	HOOKS	<.01
HATING	<.01	HOOPER	<.01
HATTER	<.01	HOOPING	<.01
HAWAIIAN	<.01	HOORAY	<.01
HAYRIDES	<.01	HOOSKERDOO	<.01
HAZZARDS	<.01	HOPING	<.01
HEADED	<.01	HORSIE	<.01
HEADER	<.01	HOTROD	<.01
HEADING	<.01	HOWE	<.01
HEADLIGHTS	<.01	HOWS*	<.01
HEALED	<.01	HUFFING	<.01
HEALTHIER	<.01	HUFFS	<.01
HEALTHY	<.01	HUGGA	<.01
HEARED*	<.01	HUNGRIER	<.01
HEARING	<.01	HUNSAKER	<.01
HEATHERS	<.01	HUNTERS	<.01
HEAVIER	<.01	HUNTS	<.01
HEBREW	<.01	HURLS	<.01
HELIUM	<.01	HURRICANE	<.01
HELL	<.01	HURRIES	<.01
HELPER	<.01	HUSBAND'S	<.01
HELPERS	<.01	HUSH	<.01
HEM	<.01	HYDRANT	<.01
HEP	<.01	I'S	<.01

WORD	PERCENT	WORD	PERCENT
ICICLES	<.01	JO	<.01
IGNORE	<.01	JOHNNY'S	<.01
IMAGINATION	<.01	JOHNSONS	<.01
IMPERIAL	<.01	JOHNSTON	<.01
IMPORTANT	<.01	JOKERS	<.01
INCLUDING	<.01	JOLLY	<.01
INDIANA'S	<.01	JONES'	<.01
INDIVISIBLE	<.01	JOSH	<.01
INITIALS	<.01	JOY	<.01
INJURED	<.01	JOYCE	<.01
INN	<.01	JUDO	<.01
INNER	<.01	JUGGLERS	<.01
INNINGS	<.01	JUGS	<.01
INSTRUCTOR	<.01	JULY	<.01
INTERRUPTION	<.01	JUMPER	<.01
INTERSECTION	<.01	JUNCTION	<.01
INTRODUCE	<.01	JUNE'S	<.01
INVENTED	<.01	JUNGLE'S	<.01
IRIS	<.01	JUNKS	<.01
IRISH	<.01	JUSTIN	<.01
IRON	<.01	KANABLE *	<.01
ISLANDS	<.01	KANGAROO'S	<.01
ISLE	<.01	KANSAS	<.01
ITALIAN	<.01	KATE'S	<.01
ITCHING	<.01	KATHLEENA	<.01
ITCHY	<.01	KAYAKS	<.01
ITSELF	<.01	KEARNEY'S	<.01
IVY	<.01	KEEPERS	<.01
JACK-O-LANTERN'S	<.01	KENDRA	<.01
JAMBOREE	<.01	KEVIN	<.01
JAMIE'S	<.01	KICKER	<.01
JAN	<.01	KICKOFFS	<.01
JANIE	<.01	KIDNAPPERS	<.01
JAPANESE	<.01	KIDNAPPING	<.01
JARS	<.01	KIDNEY	<.01
JASONS	<.01	KIKI'S	<.01
JEALOUS	<.01	KITTY'S	<.01
JEAN	<.01	KNIFES	<.01
JEANNIE'S	<.01	KNIVES	<.01
JEB	<.01	KOALA	<.01
JEFF'S	<.01	KOJAK	<.01
JEKYLL	<.01	KONG'S	<.01
JENNY'S	<.01	KOOL-AID	<.01
JERK	<.01	KOREAN	<.01
JERKED	<.01	LABORATORY	<.01
JESSICA	<.01	LABRADOR	<.01
JIMONY	<.01	LAMB	<.01
JINGLE	<.01	LANDSLIDE	<.01
JJ	<.01	LANE	<.01
JJ'S	<.01	LASER	<.01

WORD	PERCENT	WORD	PERCENT
LASERS	<.01	LUMPS	<.01
LASSO	<.01	LUNCHROOM	<.01
LASSOED	<.01	LURKEY	<.01
LASTS	<.01	LYNN	<.01
LAVERTY	<.01	M'S	<.01
LAWYER	<.01	MACDONALD	<.01
LEADED	<.01	MADDER	<.01
LEAKED	<.01	MAE	<.01
LEAKING	<.01	MAG	<.01
LEANED	<.01	MAGAZINES	<.01
LEDERLE	<.01	MAGGIE	<.01
LEGO'S	<.01	MAGNET	<.01
LEIFIE	<.01	MAGNETS	<.01
LESSON	<.01	MAILMAN	<.01
LEWIS	<.01	MAINE	<.01
LIAR	<.01	MALPH	<.01
LIBBY	<.01	MALPH'S	<.01
LIDS	<.01	MAMMY	<.01
LIED	<.01	MANAGER	<.01
LIES	<.01	MANAGERS	<.01
LIFEGUARD	<.01	MANHOLE	<.01
LIGHTER	<.01	MANNIX	<.01
LIKING	<.01	MANTIS	<.01
LIMBERLOST	<.01	MAP	<.01
LIMIT	<.01	MAPLE	<.01
LINED	<.01	MARCHED	<.01
LINING	<.01	MARIA	<.01
LINUS	<.01	MARIE'S	<.01
LIONEL	<.01	MARINO	<.01
LIP'S	<.01	MARKED	<.01
LIST	<.01	MARKER	<.01
LISTENS	<.01	MARKERS	<.01
LIVER	<.01	MARKY	<.01
LOGGERS	<.01	MARSH	<.01
LOGS	<.01	MARSH'S	<.01
LONDON	<.01	MARTIN	<.01
LONELY	<.01	MARVIN	<.01
LOOKOUT	<.01	MARX	<.01
LOOKY	<.01	MASHING	<.01
LORD	<.01	MASKED	<.01
LORI'S	<.01	MASTERPIECE	<.01
LOSED	<.01	MAT	<.01
LOTION	<.01	MATCHBOX	<.01
LOUIE	<.01	MATS	<.01
LOUISIANA	<.01	MATTHEW	<.01
LOWEST	<.01	MAXINE	<.01
LUCKIER	<.01	MCBROOMS'S	<.01
LUKE'S	<.01	ME'S*	<.01
LULLABYE	<.01	MEACHUM	<.01
LUMP	<.01	MEAL	<.01

WORD	PERCENT	WORD	PERCENT
MEANEST	<.01	MUSCADREO	<.01
MEANESTEST*	<.01	MUSHY	<.01
MEANIE	<.01	MUSTACHE	<.01
MEASURE	<.01	MUSTARD	<.01
MEASURED	<.01	MUTT	<.01
MEASURING	<.01	MUTUAL	<.01
MEATBALLS	<.01	MYSTERIES	<.01
MEATLOAF	<.01	MYSTERIOUS	<.01
MEDAL	<.01	MYTH	<.01
MEDIUM'S	<.01	NAPKIN	<.01
MEETED*	<.01	NATIONAL	<.01
MEGAPUNCH	<.01	NATIVES	<.01
MEGAPUNCHES	<.01	NATURALLY	<.01
MELODY	<.01	NEARLY	<.01
MEMORIZED	<.01	NECKLACES	<.01
MESSAGES	<.01	NEEDLE	<.01
MEXICO	<.01	NEIL	<.01
MICHELLE'S	<.01	NESS	<.01
MICK	<.01	NESTS	<.01
MIDAS	<.01	NEWSPAPERS	<.01
MIKE'S	<.01	NIBBLED	<.01
MILEAGE	<.01	NICELY	<.01
MILKED	<.01	NICER	<.01
MINIBIKING	<.01	NICKEL	<.01
MINUS	<.01	NICKELS	<.01
MIRROR	<.01	NICKLE	<.01
MIRRORS	<.01	NICKNAME	<.01
MISSION	<.01	NICKNAMES	<.01
MISSISSINEWA	<.01	NIECE	<.01
MISSY'S	<.01	NIGHT'S	<.01
MISTY	<.01	NIGHTGOWN	<.01
MOMO	<.01	NIMBLE	<.01
MONICA	<.01	NINETEENTH	<.01
MONTICELLO	<.01	NIP	<.01
MOORE	<.01	NONNIE	<.01
MOORING	<.01	NOODLES	<.01
MOPPING	<.01	NORFEL	<.01
MOSEY	<.01	NORTHWESTERN	<.01
MOTHS	<.01	NOTHINGS	<.01
MOTORBOAT	<.01	NOVA	<.01
MOUSE'S	<.01	NOWHERE	<.01
MOUSEKETEER	<.01	NUEVE	<.01
MOUSES*	<.01	NUMBER'S	<.01
MOUTH'S	<.01	NUMBERED	<.01
MUFFLER	<.01	OCHO	<.01
MUFFLERS	<.01	OCTOPUSES	<.01
MUMBLE	<.01	OHIO	<.01
MUMMIES	<.01	OLIVIA	<.01
MUMPS	<.01	OLYMPIA	<.01
MUNSTER	<.01	OMAHA	<.01

WORD	PERCENT	WORD	PERCENT
OMELET	<.01	PEACE	<.01
OOPS	<.01	PEACOCK	<.01
OPENER	<.01	PEACOCKS	<.01
OPPOSITE	<.01	PEAR	<.01
ORDER	<.01	PECK	<.01
ORDERS	<.01	PECKING	<.01
ORGAN	<.01	PECKS	<.01
OSTMAN'S	<.01	PEEK	<.01
OSTRICH	<.01	PELICAN	<.01
OUTDOOR	<.01	PENALTIES	<.01
OUTLINE	<.01	PENALTY	<.01
OUTSIDE'S	<.01	PENNIES	<.01
PACKERS	<.01	PEPE	<.01
PAGE'S	<.01	PEPPERS	<.01
PAM	<.01	PER	<.01
PAM'S	<.01	PERFUMES	<.01
PAMPA'S	<.01	PERU	<.01
PAMPAS	<.01	PETALS	<.01
PAN'S	<.01	PETE'S	<.01
PANAMA	<.01	PETRY	<.01
PANDAS	<.01	PHIL	<.01
PANE	<.01	PHONE'S	<.01
PAPAYA	<.01	PICKUP	<.01
PARCHISI	<.01	PICNICKING	<.01
PARDELL	<.01	PILES	<.01
PARENT	<.01	PILLS	<.01
PARKED	<.01	PINCHING	<.01
PARKER	<.01	PINE	<.01
PARKER'S	<.01	PINEAPPLE	<.01
PARKS	<.01	PINGBALL*	<.01
PARLOR	<.01	PITCHER'S	<.01
PART'S	<.01	PITCHERS	<.01
PARTICULAR	<.01	PITTSBURGH	<.01
PARTNER'S	<.01	PLA-DOH	<.01
PASQUALLE'S	<.01	PLANETARIUM	<.01
PASSAGE	<.01	PLANNED	<.01
PASSENGERS	<.01	PLATEFUL	<.01
PASTING	<.01	PLATTER	<.01
PASTOR	<.01	PLAY'S	<.01
PAT'S	<.01	PLAYFUL	<.01
PATHS	<.01	PLAYPEN	<.01
PATROLLING	<.01	PLAYTIME	<.01
PATTED	<.01	PLEDGE	<.01
PATTERN	<.01	PLOP	<.01
PATTING	<.01	PLUMB	<.01
PATTY'S	<.01	PLUNGER	<.01
PAULMAN'S	<.01	PLUNK	<.01
PAW	<.01	PLUNKED*	<.01
PAWNS	<.01	PLUTOS	<.01
PAYMENTS	<.01	PLYMOUTH	<.01

WORD	PERCENT	WORD	PERCENT
POCKETBOOK	<.01	PROFESSORS	<.01
POCKETFUL	<.01	PROJECTOR	<.01
POEMS	<.01	PRONOUNCE	<.01
POG	<.01	PROOF	<.01
POHLMAN	<.01	PROPELLER	<.01
POINTING	<.01	PROTECTS	<.01
POINTY	<.01	PUERTO RICO	<.01
POKED	<.01	PUFFING	<.01
POKER	<.01	PUMPED	<.01
POLICEMAN'S	<.01	PUMPER	<.01
POLICEMEN'S	<.01	PUMPS	<.01
POM	<.01	PUNISH	<.01
POMS	<.01	PUPPY'S	<.01
PONTIAC	<.01	PURPLES	<.01
PONTOON	<.01	PUSSY	<.01
PONY'S	<.01	PUZZLE'S	<.01
POOCHIE	<.01	PX	<.01
POOH'S	<.01	Q	<.01
POOLS	<.01	QUACKY	<.01
POOP	<.01	QUART	<.01
POOPED	<.01	QUATRO	<.01
POP'S	<.01	QUEENS	<.01
POPSICLE	<.01	QUICKEST	<.01
PORTABLE	<.01	QUICKSAND	<.01
POSITION	<.01	QUIETEST	<.01
POSTER	<.01	QUITS	<.01
POSTMAN	<.01	QUITTED*	<.01
POTTIES	<.01	QUITTING	<.01
POUNDS	<.01	RABBIT'S	<.01
POURS	<.01	RACER'S	<.01
POWERS	<.01	RACERS	<.01
PRACTICED	<.01	RADIOS	<.01
PRAY	<.01	RAINS	<.01
PRAYED	<.01	RAISED	<.01
PRAYING	<.01	RAKED	<.01
PREACH	<.01	RAM	<.01
PRETENDING	<.01	RAMBLING	<.01
PRETTIER	<.01	RAMPARTS	<.01
PRETTIEST	<.01	RANGE	<.01
PRETZELS	<.01	RARE	<.01
PREVIEW	<.01	RARELY	<.01
PRINCESS'	<.01	RASCAL	<.01
PRINCESSES	<.01	RATS	<.01
PRINGLE	<.01	RATTLING	<.01
PRISONER	<.01	RAYLENE	<.01
PRIVATE	<.01	READERS	<.01
PROBLEM	<.01	REBA	<.01
PRODUCED	<.01	REBEL	<.01
PRODUCTION	<.01	REBUILD	<.01
PROFESSION	<.01	RECORDED	<.01

WORD	PERCENT	WORD	PERCENT
RECORDERS	<.01	ROCKFORD	<.01
RED-TAILED	<.01	ROCKY	<.01
RED'S	<.01	RODACK	<.01
REDEYES	<.01	ROG	<.01
REEL	<.01	RONA	<.01
REFRESHMENTS	<.01	ROOFING	<.01
REINS	<.01	ROPED	<.01
RELAX	<.01	ROSE	<.01
RELAXING	<.01	ROUGH'S	<.01
RELEASE	<.01	ROUNDED	<.01
REMEMBERS	<.01	ROWED	<.01
REMIND	<.01	ROWS	<.01
REMO'S	<.01	RUBBLES	<.01
REPAIR	<.01	RUDY	<.01
REPEATS	<.01	RUNAWAY	<.01
RERUNS	<.01	RUNG	<.01
RESCUERS	<.01	RUSSIAVILLE	<.01
RESCUES	<.01	SACKS	<.01
RESCUING	<.01	SACRED	<.01
RESPECT	<.01	SADDLE	<.01
RESPONSIBILITY	<.01	SADDLES	<.01
RESTED	<.01	SAFARI	<.01
RESTING	<.01	SAIL	<.01
RESTROOM	<.01	SAILING	<.01
RETRIEVER	<.01	SAILS	<.01
REVERSES	<.01	SALE	<.01
REWARD	<.01	SAM'S	<.01
REX	<.01	SANCTUARY	<.01
RHYME	<.01	SANDPILE	<.01
RIBBON	<.01	SANDS	<.01
RIBS	<.01	SAUCERS	<.01
RICHARD	<.01	SAWED	<.01
RICKETY	<.01	SAWFISH	<.01
RICKY'S	<.01	SAWS	<.01
RIDDLE	<.01	SCALES	<.01
RIDER	<.01	SCANNER	<.01
RIDERS	<.01	SCAR	<.01
RINGED	<.01	SCARIEST	<.01
RINGING	<.01	SCATTERS	<.01
RINK	<.01	SCENES	<.01
RIP	<.01	SCHEDULE	<.01
RIPE	<.01	SCOOTED	<.01
ROAR	<.01	SCOPE	<.01
ROBBERING*	<.01	SCORED	<.01
ROBBINS	<.01	SCOUTS	<.01
ROBES	<.01	SCRAPED	<.01
ROBIN'S	<.01	SCRATCHING	<.01
ROBINSON	<.01	SCRATCHY	<.01
ROBINSON'S	<.01	SCRIBBLE	<.01
ROCKER	<.01	SCRUNCHED	<.01

WORD	PERCENT	WORD	PERCENT
SEARCH	<.01	SICKNESS	<.01
SEAWEED	<.01	SIETE	<.01
SECRETS	<.01	SIGNAL	<.01
SEIZURES	<.01	SIGNALING	<.01
SELLED*	<.01	SIGNING	<.01
SEMI	<.01	SILLS	<.01
SEMIS	<.01	SINCLAIR	<.01
SENDED*	<.01	SITE	<.01
SEPARATE	<.01	SITTED*	<.01
SERVES	<.01	SITTER'S	<.01
SES	<.01	SIX'S	<.01
SETTER	<.01	SKATEBOARD	<.01
SEVENTEENTH	<.01	SKATERS	<.01
SEWERS	<.01	SKI	<.01
SHACK	<.01	SKIDDED	<.01
SHADOWS	<.01	SKINNER	<.01
SHAFFER	<.01	SKIPPED	<.01
SHAGGY	<.01	SKIRT	<.01
SHAKES	<.01	SKIRTS	<.01
SHAKEY'S	<.01	SKIS	<.01
SHALL	<.01	SLAPPING	<.01
SHALLOW	<.01	SLAPS	<.01
SHARED*	<.01	SLEDGE	<.01
SHARPENED	<.01	SLEEPED*	<.01
SHARPENER	<.01	SLEEVES	<.01
SHAVE	<.01	SLICKY*	<.01
SHAWN'S	<.01	SLIDE'S	<.01
SHEARS	<.01	SLIME	<.01
SHEETS	<.01	SLIT	<.01
SHELFS*	<.01	SLOBBER	<.01
SHERBET	<.01	SLOPPY	<.01
SHIELDS	<.01	SLOT	<.01
SHIFT	<.01	SLOWER	<.01
SHIPPER	<.01	SLOWPOKE	<.01
SHIPWRECK	<.01	SLUD *	<.01
SHIPWRECKED	<.01	SLUMBER	<.01
SHOER	<.01	SLY	<.01
SHOOK	<.01	SMALLEST	<.01
SHORTCUTS	<.01	SMALLS	<.01
SHORTER	<.01	SMARTEST	<.01
SHORTY	<.01	SMARTY	<.01
SHORTY'S	<.01	SMASHUP	<.01
SHOTS	<.01	SMEARS	<.01
SHOVE	<.01	SMELT	<.01
SHOVEL	<.01	SMITH	<.01
SHOW-OFF	<.01	SMOOCHING	<.01
SHOWERS	<.01	SMOTHER	<.01
SHRINKING	<.01	SMURPHETTE	<.01
SHRUNK	<.01	SNAILS	<.01
SHUTTED*	<.01	SNAPPING	<.01

WORD	PERCENT	WORD	PERCENT
SNAPS	<.01	SPIED	<.01
SNEAKY	<.01	SPIKES	<.01
SNEEZING	<.01	SPILLS	<.01
SNIFFED	<.01	SPILT	<.01
SNIFFING	<.01	SPINNERS	<.01
SNORED	<.01	SPLASHES	<.01
SNOW'S	<.01	SPLASHING	<.01
SNOWMANS*	<.01	SPLINTER	<.01
SNOWMOBILING	<.01	SPOIL	<.01
SNOWS	<.01	SPOKE	<.01
SNUFFLE-UPAGUS	<.01	SPONGE	<.01
SNUGGER*	<.01	SPONGES	<.01
SO'S	<.01	SPOTTED	<.01
SOAK	<.01	SPRAINED	<.01
SOAKING	<.01	SPREADED*	<.01
SOCKING	<.01	SPRINGTIME	<.01
SOGGY	<.01	SPRITE	<.01
SOLES	<.01	SPRUNGED*	<.01
SOLO	<.01	SQUASHED	<.01
SOLVED	<.01	SQUEAKY	<.01
SOLVER	<.01	SQUIRTED	<.01
SOMEBODYS	<.01	STAGES	<.01
SOMEDAYS*	<.01	STAIRWAY	<.01
SOMETHINGS	<.01	STAIRWAYS	<.01
SOMEWHERES*	<.01	STAKE	<.01
SORES	<.01	STALLED	<.01
SORTS	<.01	STALLION	<.01
SOUNDED	<.01	STAMPED	<.01
SOUNDING	<.01	STAMPING	<.01
SOUNDLY	<.01	STANDED*	<.01
SOUPY	<.01	STAPLER	<.01
SOUR	<.01	STARE	<.01
SOUVENIR	<.01	STARED	<.01
SPANIEL	<.01	STARSKY'S	<.01
SPANKINGS	<.01	STARTLED	<.01
SPANKY'S	<.01	STARVE	<.01
SPARK	<.01	STEAMED	<.01
SPARKLE	<.01	STEEP	<.01
SPARKS	<.01	STEERS	<.01
SPARKY	<.01	STEVENS	<.01
SPEAKER	<.01	STICKER	<.01
SPEAKERS	<.01	STINGER	<.01
SPEAKS	<.01	STINGERS	<.01
SPEAR	<.01	STINGY	<.01
SPECTACULAR	<.01	STIR	<.01
SPEECH	<.01	STITCHING	<.01
SPEEDOMETER	<.01	STOCK	<.01
SPEEDS	<.01	STOLEN	<.01
SPELT*	<.01	STOMACH'S	<.01
SPICE	<.01	STOMPED	<.01

WORD	PERCENT	WORD	PERCENT
STOOLS	<.01	SWIRLING	<.01
STOPPER	<.01	SWISH	<.01
STOVES	<.01	SWISHED	<.01
STRANGE	<.01	SWITCHED	<.01
STRANGERS	<.01	SWITCHING	<.01
STREAKING	<.01	SWITCHMAN	<.01
STREAMS	<.01	SWOLLED*	<.01
STRETCH'S	<.01	SYLVESTER	<.01
STRIKED*	<.01	T-SHIRTS	<.01
STRINGER	<.01	TABLET	<.01
STRIPPED	<.01	TACO	<.01
STROLLER	<.01	TACO'S	<.01
STROLLERS	<.01	TADPOLE	<.01
STRON'S	<.01	TAIL'S	<.01
STRONGEST	<.01	TAMMY'S	<.01
STU	<.01	TANGLES	<.01
STUB	<.01	TARDY	<.01
STUDY	<.01	TART	<.01
STUDYING	<.01	TAXI	<.01
STUFF'S	<.01	TAXICAB	<.01
STUFFING	<.01	TEACHING	<.01
STUFFS	<.01	TEAM'S	<.01
STUMP	<.01	TEAPOTS	<.01
STUMPS	<.01	TEARED*	<.01
STURDY	<.01	TEASED	<.01
STURGESS	<.01	TEASING	<.01
STYLE	<.01	TEENAGER	<.01
SUBS	<.01	TEENAGERS	<.01
SUBSTITUTE	<.01	TEES	<.01
SUCKING	<.01	TELEPHONES	<.01
SUCTION	<.01	TENDS	<.01
SUITCASES	<.01	TENSION	<.01
SUN'S	<.01	TENTS	<.01
SUNDAES	<.01	TEPEE	<.01
SUNFISH	<.01	TERESA'S	<.01
SUNS	<.01	TESCADERO	<.01
SUNSET	<.01	THANKING	<.01
SUNSET'S	<.01	THEATER	<.01
SUPERHEROS	<.01	THEATERS	<.01
SUPERS	<.01	THEIRSELF*	<.01
SUPPER'S	<.01	THEIRSELVES*	<.01
SURPRISED	<.01	THERE'LL	<.01
SUSPECT	<.01	THICK	<.01
SWALLOWS	<.01	THINKED*	<.01
SWAMP	<.01	THIRTEENTH	<.01
SWEAT	<.01	THIRTY-ONE	<.01
SWEATING	<.01	THIS-A-WAY	<.01
SWEEPER	<.01	THREATENED	<.01
SWELL	<.01	THREES	<.01
SWELLED	<.01	THROWN	<.01

WORD	PERCENT	WORD	PERCENT
THUMB	<.01	TRICKY	<.01
THUMP	<.01	TRICYCLES	<.01
THUNDERBIRD	<.01	TRIKE	<.01
THUNK*	<.01	TROOP'S	<.01
TICK	<.01	TROPHIES	<.01
TICKLISH	<.01	TROUT	<.01
TICO	<.01	TRUCK'S	<.01
TIES	<.01	TRUTH	<.01
TIGHTER	<.01	TTP	<.01
TIME'S	<.01	TUBE	<.01
TIMED	<.01	TUGGING	<.01
TINIEST	<.01	TUNA	<.01
TIPPING	<.01	TUNE	<.01
TIPPY	<.01	TUNNELS	<.01
TIPS	<.01	TUPPERWARE	<.01
TOAD'S	<.01	TUT	<.01
TOADS	<.01	TUT'S	<.01
TODAY'S	<.01	TV'S	<.01
TOENAIL	<.01	TVS	<.01
TOM'S	<.01	TWEEZERS	<.01
TOMB	<.01	TWELFTH	<.01
TOMBSTONE	<.01	TWENTY-ONE	<.01
TOMORROW'S	<.01	TWENTY-SIX	<.01
TONGUE'S	<.01	TWENTY-SIXTH	<.01
TONGUES	<.01	TWENTY-TWO	<.01
TOOTHES	<.01	TWICEST*	<.01
TOOTSIE	<.01	TWIGLEY'S	<.01
TOPPED	<.01	TWIRLED	<.01
TORED*	<.01	TWIRLER	<.01
TORPEDO	<.01	TWO'S	<.01
TORTURES	<.01	TYPEWRITER	<.01
TOSSED	<.01	ULTRAMAN	<.01
TOTE	<.01	ULTRAMAN'S	<.01
TOTTERS	<.01	UMPING	<.01
TOUGHIE	<.01	UNBUTTONED	<.01
TOWARD	<.01	UNCOVERED	<.01
TOWARDS	<.01	UNDERSTAND	<.01
TRACE	<.01	UNDONE	<.01
TRACING	<.01	UNFREEZED*	<.01
TRACTORS	<.01	UNICORNS	<.01
TRADED	<.01	UNIFORMS	<.01
TRAFFIC	<.01	UNION	<.01
TRAPEZE	<.01	UNITED	<.01
TRAVELING	<.01	UNIVERSE	<.01
TRAVIS	<.01	UNIVERSITY	<.01
TRAY	<.01	UNLOCK	<.01
TRAYS	<.01	UNSTICKED*	<.01
TREAT	<.01	UNTAGGED*	<.01
TRES	<.01	UNTIE	<.01
TRIALS	<.01	UPHILL	<.01

WORD	PERCENT	WORD	PERCENT
UPTOWN	<.01	WHIPPINGS	<.01
USUAL	<.01	WHIRLYBIRD	<.01
VALENTINES	<.01	WHISKERS	<.01
VALERIE	<.01	WHISTLES	<.01
VAMPIRE'S	<.01	WHISTLING	<.01
VAMPIRES	<.01	WHITE'S	<.01
VASE	<.01	WHY'D	<.01
VASELINE	<.01	WILDCAT	<.01
VASES	<.01	WINDOW'S	<.01
VELMA	<.01	WINDPIPE	<.01
VERSUS	<.01	WINDY	<.01
VET	<.01	WINE	<.01
VICTOR	<.01	WINKING	<.01
VIPERS	<.01	WIPERS	<.01
VIRGINIA	<.01	WIPING	<.01
VON	<.01	WISCONSIN	<.01
WADE	<.01	WISHED	<.01
WADING	<.01	WIT	<.01
WAFFLE'S	<.01	WIVES	<.01
WAGONS	<.01	WOKED	<.01
WAKED	<.01	WOLF'S	<.01
WAKES	<.01	WOLVES	<.01
WALKER	<.01	WOMAN'S	<.01
WALLET	<.01	WOMANS	<.01
WALLPAPER'S	<.01	WOMENS*	<.01
WALTER	<.01	WONDERING	<.01
WANDERING	<.01	WONDERLAND	<.01
WARMED	<.01	WONDERWOMAN	<.01
WASHER	<.01	WONNED*	<.01
WASHER'S	<.01	WOODCUTTER	<.01
WASHES	<.01	WOODSMAN	<.01
WATERED	<.01	WOOS	<.01
WATERFALLS	<.01	WORED*	<.01
WATERING	<.01	WORRIED	<.01
WAVY	<.01	WORSE	<.01
WAYNE	<.01	WORST	<.01
WE'S*	<.01	WORSTEST*	<.01
WEAPON	<.01	WOUND	<.01
WEATHER	<.01	WRECKING	<.01
WEED	<.01	WRECKS	<.01
WEEKENDS	<.01	WRIT*	<.01
WEENSY	<.01	WRITES	<.01
WEIGHTED	<.01	WRITTEN	<.01
WEIGHTS	<.01	WUGGY	<.01
WELFARE	<.01	X'S	<.01
WESTERNS	<.01	Y'ALL'S	<.01
WESTWOOD	<.01	YABA	<.01
WHEEL'S	<.01	YARDAGE	<.01
WHEN'S	<.01	YELLOWISH	<.01
WHERE'D	<.01	YELLOWSTONE	<.01

WORD	PERCENT
YMCA	<.01
YOGURT	<.01
YOUNG	<.01
YOUNGEST	<.01
YUMMY	<.01
YWCA	<.01
Z	<.01
ZERO'S	<.01
ZEROES	<.01
ZIPPED	<.01
ZIPPING	<.01
ZOOMED	<.01

INDEX